must sees
Amsterdam

J. Subtil/MICHELIN

MICHELIN

mustsees **Amsterdam**

Editorial Manager	Jonathan P. Gilbert
Editor	Gwen Cannon
Contributing Writers	Kristen de Joseph, Vicky Hampton, Angela Rhodes
Production Manager	Natasha G. George
Cartography	John Dear
Photo Editor	Yoshimi Kanazawa
Photo Research	Nicole D. Jordan
Proofreader	Wayne H. Heath
Layout	Nicole D. Jordan, Natasha G. George
Interior Design	Chris Bell, cbdesign
Cover Design	Chris Bell, cbdesign, Natasha G. George

Contact Us

Michelin Maps and Guides
One Parkway South
Greenville, SC 29615
USA
www.michelintravel.com

Michelin Maps and Guides
Hannay House
39 Clarendon Road
Watford, Herts WD17 1JA
UK
(01923) 205 240
www.ViaMichelin.com
travelpubsales@uk.michelin.com

Special Sales

For information regarding bulk sales, customized
editions and premium sales, please contact
our Customer Service Departments:

USA	1-800-432-6277
UK	(01923) 205 240
Canada	1-800-361-8236

Michelin Apa Publications Ltd

58 Borough High Street, London SE1 1XF, United Kingdom

© 2012 Michelin Apa Publications Ltd
ISBN 978-1-907099-73-1
Printed: December 2011
Printed and bound: Himmer, Germany

Note to the reader:

Cafe by the canal, the Jordaan

Introduction

Must See

p 119

©Mats Stafseng Einarsen/Michelin

©Jochen Tack/NBTC

TABLE OF CONTENTS

★★★ ATTRACTIONS

Unmissable historic, cultural and natural sights

Rijksmuseum p 72

©Arie de Leeuw/Rijksmuseum

Van Gogh Museum p 94

©Hans Zaglitsch / age fotostock

Bulb fields of Keukenhof p 111

©NBTC

Herengracht p 51

© Amanda Hall / age fotostock

Nationaal Park de Hoge Veluwe p 109

© Hans Drijer/NP de Hoge Veluwe

Picturesque canals p 51

©Angela Rhodes/Michelin

ACTIVITIES

Unmissable activities and entertainment

Cheese galore p 126

Time tall ships p 119

Browse for books p 129

Shop the department stores, Magna Plaza p 126

MUST KNOW

Dawdle at the zoo p 120
©Artis

Wooden shoes p 129
© NBTC

Seven Bridges Hotel p 146
©Günter Glaner/Seven Bridges Hotel

Grand Hotel Amráth p 149
©Grand Hotel Amráth

★★★ ATTRACTIONS

Unmissable historic, cultural and natural sights

For more than 75 years people have used Michelin stars to take the guesswork out of travel. Our star-rating system helps you make the best decision on where to go, what to do, and what to see.

★★★	Unmissable
★★	Worth a trip
★	Worth a detour
No star	Recommended

MUST KNOW

ACTIVITIES

Unmissable activities, entertainment, restaurants and hotels

For every historic and natural sight in Amsterdam, there are many more activities. We recommend all of the activities in this guide, but our top picks are highlighted with the Michelin Man logo.

STAR ATTRACTIONS

IDEAS AND TOURS

Throughout this thematic guide you will find inspiration for many different ways to experience Amsterdam. The following is a selection to help start you off. The sights in bold are found in the index.

☞ WALKING TOURS

Amsterdam is a great place to wander around, be it the canal banks, the public squares or the city parks.
The following self-guided walking tours are tailored to the sights found in Districts.

Nieuwe Zijde★★ (New Side)

The historic heart of the city is awash in grand buildings that include its oldest churches and the Royal Palace. Its focus of history is the **Dam★**, Amsterdam's busy main square, at the intersection of two major thoroughfares, **Damrak** and Rokin. Begin in the north at **Centraal Station**, the imposing train station that occupies three artificial islands in the IJ River, and walk south to Dam square. Overlooking it are **Nieuwe Kerk★★**, the national church of the Netherlands where

the country's sovereigns are crowned, and **Koninklijk Paleis★**, the Royal Palace, a monumental Classical-style building erected on 13,659 wooden piles. Just east is **Madame Tussauds**, where audio-animatronics bring to life Amsterdam's Golden Age (the 1600s). Continue south on Kalverstraat to the **Amsterdam Museum★★**, where exhibits trace the history of the city chronologically and thematically. Nearby, the **Begijnhof★★**, founded in the 14C, is one of the few remaining convents in the Netherlands. Continue to the **Singel★★** canal, at the southwest end of Kalverstraat, and follow it to the city's colorful **Bloemenmarkt★★**, where cut flowers, bulbs and souvenirs are for sale. Sitting between the Singel and the Amstel River is the **Muntplein**, with its Mint Tower, the place to end your walk.

Dam square

©ATCB

MUST KNOW

Oude Zijde★★ (Old Side)

The old side of the city center encompasses Waterlooplein, the former Jewish area, Nieuwmarkt and the Red-Light District. Begin in the square known as the **Waterlooplein**, east of Muntplein, but on the opposite side of the Amstel River. The **Stopera**, a modern complex, houses the **Muziektheater** and city hall. Opposite stands the house of the famous painter Rembrandt, now the **Museum Het Rembrandthuis★**. East of the Waterlooplein lies the **Jodenbuurt**, the former Jewish quarter. Highlights include the **Joods Historisch Museum★**, in which exhibits on Jewish identity are showcased; the **Portugees-Israëlitische Synagoge★**, a massive building (1675) erected as a place of worship for Portuguese congregations; and the **Pintohuis**, a 17C patrician mansion of a well-to-do Portuguese-Jewish family. Walk north past Rembrandt's house to the Renaissance-style **Zuiderkerk** (1611), the first church in Amsterdam built especially for Protestant services. Continue north to **Nieuwmarkt**, a favorite spot with terraced cafes. **De Waag** (the Weighing House) rises over the square. Just west of Nieuwmarkt lies the **Walletjes★★**, Amsterdam's notorious red-light district, which comes alive at night. West of the canal at Oudezijds Voorburgwal rises the oldest church in the city, the **Oude Kerk★★** built in 1306. At the north end of the canal, the domed neo-Baroque **Sint Nicolaaskerk** was built in 1887 for Catholics. Continue north to end your tour at Centraal Station.

De Pijp

Known as the "Latin Quarter" of Amsterdam, where you will see all walks of life, De Pijp lies south of city center and east of the Van Gogh Museum. De Pijp is Dutch for "The Pipe." The neighborhood was possibly named for its long, narrow streets that are actually filled-in canals. Usually associated with major tourist sights like the Heineken Experience and the Albert Cuyp market, it is also brimming with cafes, restaurants, shops—and a cosmopolitan buzz. The peaceful park called **Sarphatipark** dominates its center. Begin your walking tour in the afternoon at the **Albert Cuypmarkt★**, a colorful market in existence since 1904 that sells everything from fruit to clothing from around the globe. You may want to buy picnic food to take two blocks south to nearby Sarphatipark for an alfresco lunch. Head west to Ferdinand Bolstraat and turn north toward the Singelgracht canal to find the **Heineken Experience** *(last ticket sales 5:30pm)* on the corner at Stadhouderskade. The famed brewery was built in 1864; a tour highlights the company's history and brewing methods, and ends with a free sample of beer.

The next street south, Tweede Jacob van Campenstraat, leads back to the Albert Cuypmarkt via Eerste Sweelinckstraat. End your walking tour with dinner and live music at **Badcuyp Centrum voor Muziek** (Badcuyp Center for Music) at Eerste Sweelinckstraat 10, where reasonably priced meals are served every day except Monday.

IDEAS AND TOURS

BOAT TOURS

Amsterdam's four concentric **canals★★★**—the **Singel★★,** the **Herengracht★★★**, the **Keizersgracht★★** and the **Prinsengracht★★** to the west and south of the historic town center—have been flowing since the 17C, and the Singel a bit earlier than that. A **boat tour** offers an excellent view of the most important canals as well as part of the port; most of the standard tours last about one hour. The route varies according to which locks are open. *For a tour, contact any of the following operators:*

Rederij Lovers, Prins Hendrikkade 25, 020 530 1090, www.lovers.nl
Rederij Kooij, opposite Rokin 125, 020 623 3810, www.rederjkooij.nl
Gray Line Amsterdam, Damrak Steiger 5, 020 535 3308, www.graylineamsterdam.com
Amsterdam Canal Cruises, Stadhouderskade 550, 020 626 5636, www.amsterdamcanal cruises.nl.

BIKE TRIPS

Amsterdam is said to have more than half a million bicycles. Cycling is ideal transportion for a low-lying, flat land devoid of hills. Bike paths abound in the city. Below are three **suggested tours** that begin and end at Centraal Station.

Tour 1: Historic Old Town *45min.*

From the station, take Spuistraat (west of Damrak, but east of the Singel canal). At the end of this long street, follow the Singel, which extends briefly into the Amstel River beyond Muntplein. Cross the first bridge on the left (Halvemaansbrug) and turn sharp right into 's-Gravelandseveer. Turn into Groenburgwal and at the end, turn right and continue along the Raamgracht to the end. Backtrack along the opposite side of the Raamgracht, then turn into Moddermolenstraat, the second street on the right. Cross Zuiderkerkhof and Sint Antoniesbreestraat, then turn into the narrow Snoekjessteeg. Bear left and skirt the Krom Boomssloot, at the end of which you should turn right into Recht Boomsloot. Turn left into Oudeschans and return to the station via Binnenkant, which runs along the Waalseilandsgracht.

After the long Spuistraat, the road crosses the **Spui** before following the last section of the **Singel★★**, one side of which is taken up by the **Bloemenmarkt★★**. The road junction on **Muntplein** is a crossroads used by pedestrians, cyclists, tramways and cars, so be alert. The next section is full of more bends and corners. This area is the old town of Amsterdam. The canals are shorter and narrower. You will cycle past the **Zuiderkerk** and the **Oudeschans★**, a canal named for the former defensive wall on this site. The round trip encompasses **Oosterdok** and two of its sights: the **Scheepvaarthuis★**, or 1916 shipping house (now a hotel) and the **Schreierstoren**, a 15C semi-circular tower, before returning to Centraal Station.

Tour 2: Westerdok, Westerpark and Brouwersgracht

45min. Cycle around Centraal Station and head west on the De

Ruijterkade, then go right over the bridge to the Westerdoksdijk. Turn left into Barentszplein and Van Diemenstraat. Beyond no. 6, follow the narrow passage that runs along the Van Diemenkade warehouses. Pick up the bike path again and turn into Tasmanstraat beyond the Westerkanaal. Turn right into Stavangerweg and right again into Haparandaweg. Follow Danzigerkade and Minervahavenweg, then return to Haparandaweg and go left into Archangelweg.

After following the **IJ** River, then the **Westerdok** and the **Barentszplein**, the route takes you past **Amsterdam Harbor**. Actually, the harbor made famous by Jacques Brel's song is not accessible to nonprofessionals, and is now the North Sea Canal. The barges on Van Diemenkade and Danzigerkade gradually give way to tug boats and huge ships in the Westpoort harbor area.

Cross the Spaarndammerdijk and head to the right, then turn left into Zaanstraat. At the end of the street, turn right under the railway bridge (on a level with Zaandijkstraat) and once you reach Westerpark, turn left. At the park exit, turn right then left at the traffic lights. On Haarlemmerplein, turn right into Nieuwe Wagenstraat and left along the Brouwersgracht canal. Return to the station via Prins Hendrikkade.

On Zaanstraat rises **Het Schip★**, an apartment block by the **Amsterdam School** *(see Architecture)*.

On leaving Westerpark, note the Haarlemmerpoort, a neo-Classical gate built in 1840. The tour takes in the **Brouwersgracht**, a delightful canal whatever the weather.

Tour 3: Western, Southern and Eastern Outer Canals *1hr 15 min.*

Western Outer Canals – From the station, head for the north end of Prinsengracht. Cycle along its banks (even-numbered side) and turn right to the Bloemgracht. Cross the Lijnbaansgracht at the end and turn left into Marnixstraat. This street skirts the Lijnbaansgracht. At Kinkerstraat (on the right), turn left then right to cycle along the other side of the Lijnbaansgracht. Turn left onto the Looiersgracht and at the end, right onto the banks of the Prinsengracht. Turn right on the Leidsegracht.

From this section of the **Prinsengracht★★**, where many houseboats are moored, there is a good **view** of the bell tower on Westerkerk. Beyond the delightful **Bloemgracht** is Marnixstraat, from which you can see the Singelgracht on the right. This less picturesque route shows the extent to which canals continue to rule the urban geography, even far from city center.

Southern Outer Canals – At the end of the Leidsegracht, turn left along the Lijnbaansgracht. Cross Leidseplein (watch out for trams), turn into Weteringschans, then right on Museumbrug. Opposite the Rijksmuseum, turn right, then left and cycle along the Stadhouderskade. Opposite the Heineken building, turn left, cross the square and follow the Vijzelgracht. Then turn right along the Lijnbaansgracht. At the end, cross the bridge, turn left along the Reguliersgracht, then right along the Prinsengracht. This tour is a return to the tranquility of the **Leidsegracht**, beyond which is a short stretch of the Lijnbaansgracht. Here you can see **Melkweg** and then the bustling **Leidseplein★**. Beyond the **Paradiso** is the **Rijksmuseum★★★**, the city's renowned art museum, and the **Heineken Brouwerij**, Holland's famed brewery. The tour also takes in the **Reguliersgracht★**, and the **Prinsengracht★★**.

Eastern Outer Canals – At the end of the Prinsengracht, turn left then right onto the Magere Brug. Beyond it, turn left and right along the Nieuwe Keizersgracht. At the end, turn right into Roetersstraat, then left onto Nieuwe Prinsengracht (private road). Dismount before passing the chicane and crossing the pedestrian bridge over the canal. Turn right along the Plantage Muidergracht, then left into Plantage Middenlaan. Beyond Artis, turn right into Plantage Kerklaan and head for Entrepotdok. On the Entrepotdok turn left toward Kadijksplein.

Return to the station via the Prins Hendrikkade.

The **Magere Brug★** over the Amstel runs past the **Amstelhof**, (now home to the **Hermitage Amsterdam★★**, see Museums), the university campus and the Plantage Muidergracht, on which barges moor, not far from the **Muiderpoort**, the gate (1771) through which Napoleon entered the city. Beyond **Artis★★** (see For Kids) lies the **Entrepotdok**, whose former 17C and 18C warehouses have been converted to offices, cafes and housing. Take a break here before returning to the station.

MARKETS

Even if you don't buy anything, the city's markets are a great place to people-watch. But the markets are too far flung to make a walking tour of them. Plan to visit one or two during your stay. Here are some of Amsterdam's daily and weekly markets.

Albert Cuypmarkt★ – *Albert Cuypstraat; Mon–Sat 9am–5pm.* Occupying the same two-mile-long street since 1904 in the De Pijp neighborhood, this well-known markets sells general goods, clothing, produce and foodstuffs from around the world.

Bloemenmarkt★★
Singel canal, between Muntplein and Koningsplein; Mon–Sat 9am–5:30pm, Sun 11am–5:30pm. Located at the southern end of the Singel canal, this colorful flower market has existed since 1862. Cut flowers, bulbs, plants as well as clogs and other souvenirs entice passers-by as well as shoppers.

Nieuwmarkt – **In Oude Zijde, at the north end of the Kloveniersburgwal**. Nieuwmarkt

Magere Brug

©ATCB

is the site of a **daily market** (*Mon–Sat 9am–6pm, Sun til 5pm*), which sells foodstuffs, and on Sunday, art, antiques and books.

Noordermarkt – *In the Jordaan, west of the Prinsengracht.* Noordermarkt is the site of the weekly **Boerenmarkt** (*Sat 9am–6pm; www.boerenmarkt amsterdam.nl*), the country's first farmer's market and now an Amsterdam institution; organic fruits and vegetables are for sale. On Mondays there is a **general market.**

Waterlooplein – *Along the Amstel River at Zwanenburgwal. Mon–Sat 9am–5pm.* This large square is the setting for a lively **flea market** that offers second-hand clothes and furniture, ethnic jewelry, textiles and other wares for sale.

SIDE TRIPS

Given the capital city's somewhat central location in the northern half of the country, several interesting towns and attractions are not far away. It is highly recommended that you take at least a couple of side trips to tourist sights lying outside Amsterdam, best seen by car, although tour buses and public transportation are available to many of them.

Here are suggestions to get your planning started: the old city of **Haarlem★★**; the Netherland's chief **tulip-bulb fields★★★** around **Keukenhof★★**; the city of **Delft★★** and its famous delftware; the cheese market of **Alkmaar★**; the 19 windmills of **Kinderdijk★★**; and the villages of **Volendam★** and **Marken★**, where traditional dress is still worn. For descriptions of these sights, *see Just A Jaunt Away.*

Quick Trips
Stuck for ideas? Try these:

IDEAS AND TOURS

CALENDAR OF EVENTS

Listed below is a selection of Amsterdam's most popular annual events (dates and times vary; check in advance). *For more details telephone, or access online, the Amsterdam Tourism & Convention Board: (31) 020 201 8800 or www.iamsterdam.com.*

January/February
Chinese New Year

Held usually in late January or early February, Amsterdam's Chinese New Year celebrations take place in Nieuwmarkt's Chinatown. Festivities include street parades and parties, lion dances, gongs and firecrackers.

March/April
Restaurant Week

www.restaurantweek.nl
Twice a year in March and September participating Amsterdam restaurants offer a three-course menu at an affordable cost. The event provides diners an opportunity to try the dishes of Amsterdam's best restaurants at wallet-pleasing prices. Restaurants vary from each year. Book online.

April: Koninginnedag (Queen's Day)
©ATCB

National Museum Weekend

www.museumweekend.nl
Early to mid-April sees more than 500 museums countrywide open their doors to the public at discounted prices or free of charge. Several of the museums also offer special events during this weekend.

Imagine Film Festival

www.imaginefilmfestival.nl
Formerly known as the Amsterdam Fantastic Film Festival, this extravaganza of international and local fantasy, science fiction, cult, horror and animation films takes place during April.

Koninginnedag (Queen's Day)

On April 30 every year (unless it falls on a Sunday), Queen's Day commemorates the birthday of the Queen Mother. Amsterdam's largest open-air event draws locals and more than 800,000 visitors. The city becomes one huge street party with live music, DJs, decorated canal boats and a city-wide flea market. Celebrations begin with Koninginnenacht (Queen's Night) the night before.

May/June
National Remembrance Day

On May 4 the Netherlands pay their respects to the fallen soldiers of World War II by observing two minutes of silence at 8pm following the laying of a wreath at the National

Monument in Amsterdam by Queen Beatrix.

Liberation Day

May 5 commemorates the end of German occupation in the Netherlands in 1945.

The day is remembered with speeches and live music in several of Amsterdam's parks and squares.

National Mill Day

Each year on the second Saturday in May, the Netherlands observes National Mill Day in honor of the vital machines that have helped the nation's development. Hundreds of windmills and watermills throughout the country are opened to the public; most host special activities and shows.

Vondelpark Open Air Theater

www.openluchtteater.nl

Beginning in June, this three-month program features all genres of music, dance, theater and stand-up comedy performed on a large outdoor stage in popular Vondelpark *(see Parks and Gardens)*. Entry is free, but donations are appreciated.

Open Garden Days

www.opentuinendagen.nl

Every year on the third weekend of June, about 30 gardens hidden behind some of Amsterdam's most beautiful canal houses can be viewed by the public. One of Amsterdam's best kept secrets, many of them are private gardens.

Amsterdam Roots Festival

www.amsterdamroots.nl

This music festival is held in late June and features world music from local and international artists as well as workshops, markets and global foods.

Events are hosted at several locations.

Holland Festival

www.hollandfestival.nl

A month-long festival in June, this major annual event devoted to international performing arts showcases some of the world's most celebrated composers, concerts, operas, dances, theater and films. Performances are held in several venues around Amsterdam.

Comedytrain International Festival

www.toomler.nl

This annual comedy festival rolls into town at the end of June and spotlights stand-up comedians from Australia, Ireland, the US, the UK and Canada. All performances are in English and are hosted by the Toomler comedy club.

International Theatre School Festival Amsterdam - ITs

www.itsfestivalamsterdam.com

Late June every year students from local and international theater schools present their work in front of public audiences, casting agents, directors and members of the press. Performances include dance, theater, mime and music that are presented in several theaters around Amsterdam.

July/August

Julidans

www.julidans.nl

Held every summer, this popular international contemporary dance festival features some of the world's best choreographers and performers. Expect cutting-edge productions and a preview of next-generation modern works in Julidans NEXT program. The event takes place in July throughout the city.

Keti Koti Festival

www.ketikotiamsterdam.nl
Occurring every July 1, this free music and cultural event celebrates the end of slavery in 1863 in the former Dutch colonies, two of which, Suriname and the Antilles, are the focus of the festival.

De Parade

www.deparade.nl
Held annually in August, this traveling theater festival showcases more than 80 different performances of theater, dance and music staged in Amsterdam's Martin Luther King Park.

Grachtenfestival

www.grachtenfestival.nl
Translated as "canal festival," this yearly August event highlights performances of classical music along, as well as on, Amsterdam's canals and rivers.

Open Air Film Festival

www.plukdenacht.nl
Pluk de Nacht (Seize the Night) is a free outdoor cinema festival held in mid-August every year. Showings include not yet released independent and art house films, animation and shorts as well as documentaries.

Uitmarkt

www.amsterdamsuitburo.nl/uitmarkt
This cultural event kicks off Amsterdam's cultural season the last weekend in August. Uitmarkt hosts free music, theater and dance performances in several genres. Held in many locations around Amsterdam, the event includes a book market, workshops and more.

September/October

Open Monument Days (Heritage Days)

www.openmonumentendag.nl
On the second weekend of the month of September, thousands of historical sites and buildings nationwide that are usually closed to the public open their doors.

Jordaan Festival

www.jordaanfestival.nl
Held in mid-September, the Jordaan Festival celebrates the

July: Julidans— Southern Comfort performance

©John Hogg/Julidans

September: *Taste of Amsterdam*

©Taste of Amsterdam

neighborhood's rich history with a free street party. Festivities include drum bands, cabaret, opera and sing-alongs.

Taste of Amsterdam
www.tasteofamsterdam.com
Every September Amstelpark hosts this open-air festival of culinary delights. Attendees meet with Amsterdam's top chefs to sample their signature dishes, learn about fine wines, see live demonstrations, pick up treats at the fine food market and other activities.

Amsterdam Marathon
www.amsterdammarathon.nl
Held annually in October, the Amsterdam Marathon attracts thousands of runners who participate in a number of races.

November/December

International Documentary Film Festival Amsterdam
www.idfa.nl
Every year in November, Amsterdam hosts one of the world's leading documentary film festivals. Screenings include films from both local and international documentary filmmakers.

Museum Night
www.n8.nl
One day a year in November, several of Amsterdam's museums stay open throughout the night. In addition to their normal exhibitions, many of them host workshops, tours, concerts and performances. Museumkaart and I amsterdam City Card do not apply.

Pan Amsterdam
www.pan.nl
This annual art, antiques and design fair is always scheduled in November and held at the city's mammoth RAI (convention center). The event combines modern and contemporary art and design with objects from the past.

Sinterklaas
The official arrival of St. Nicholas is heralded on the third Sunday before December 5 as he sails into Amsterdam on a boat. Then striding his white horse, he leads a parade. On December 5, St. Nicholas' eve, he is celebrated with the exchange of gifts.

PRACTICAL INFORMATION

WHEN TO GO

Amsterdam lies in northcentral Netherlands. The city sits 2m/6.5ft above sea level between the IJ River to the north and the River Amstel, which flows into the metropolis from the south. Because of its proximity to the North Sea, Amsterdam has a **maritime climate** that ensures mild winters and cool summers, making it a year-round destination. Light rain occurs throughout the year; Amsterdam averages 186 rainy days and roughly 833mm of precipitation annually.

Peak tourist season is June to August in Amsterdam. It's the best time to enjoy sunshine and pleasant temperatures averaging 20-22°C/67-72°F. During these months the city comes alive with festivals and events such as the Holland Festival and Vondelpark's Open Air Theater. On Queen's Day (April 30), celebrating the Queen's birthday, the city erupts in a sea of orange with street parties, outdoor performances and live music, and flea markets. If your visit coincides with these events, it is highly advisable to book accommodations early, as hotel rooms fill up very quickly.

Winter often sees some snowfall; temperatures hover around freezing in January and February.

Spring can be windy. Mid-April to the end of May is a colorful time to arrive: the city's flowers and trees are beginning to bloom, and the tulips start to come out. An ideal time to visit Keukenhof is toward the end of April. **Summer** rarely gets very hot; highs usually average 20°C. Daylight lasts an average of 17 hours, permitting plenty of outdoor activities. Bicycle and foot are the best ways to explore the city.

KNOW BEFORE YOU GO
Useful Websites

www.iamsterdam.com
Official website of the Amsterdam Tourism & Convention Board with information on events, museums and other attractions, shopping, dining and hotels.

www.timeoutamsterdam.com
Amsterdam edition of this online magazine lists events, entertainment, restaurants, gigs and clubs.

www.gvb.nl/english
Amsterdam's public transport company has information and timetables on the cities integrated tram, metro and bus services.

www.holland.com/global/ Tourism.htm – Official website of the Netherlands Bureau for tourism and conventions has information specific to Amsterdam such as

Average Seasonal Temperatures in Amsterdam			
	Jan	**Apr**	**Jul**	**Oct**
Avg. High	5°C/41°F	12°C/54°F	21°C/70°F	14°C/58°F
Avg. Low	1°C/34°F	4°C/39°F	13°C/56°F	7°C/45°F

Source: www.iamsterdam.com

Tourist Information Office

HOTEL & TOURIST INFORMATION

amsterdam tourist office

NOORD-ZUID HOLLANDSCH KOFFIEHUIS

©ATCB

attractions, shopping, canals, architecture and more.

www.government.nl – The official website of the government of the Netherlands, featuring news, information about the government and topics A-Z.

www.amsterdam.nl – Official website of the City of Amsterdam with features on entertainment, news briefs, festivals, government services *(in Dutch)*.

Tourism Offices

www.iamsterdam.com – Amsterdam's main tourist information office is located at Stationsquare across from Centraal Station, Stationsplein 10, *31 (0)20 201 8800.*

Holland's Tourist Information can be found at Schipol Plaza at the Schipol Airport, Arrivals Hall 2, *31 (0)20 201 8800.*

International Visitors
Netherlands Embassies Abroad

Canada – Embassy of the Kingdom of the Netherlands. 2020-350 Albert Street, Ottawa, *1-877-388-2443, http://ottawa. the-netherlands.org*

US – Royal Netherlands Embassy. 4200 Linnean Avenue NW, Washington, *1-877-388-2443, http://dc.the-netherlands.org*

UK – Embassy of the Kingdom of the Netherlands. 38 Hyde Park Gate, London SW7 5DP, United Kingdom, *0044 (0)20 7590 3200, www.dutchembassyuk.org*

Foreign Embassies and Consulates

Australian Embassy – Carnegielaan 4, 2517 KH The Hague, *31 (0)70 310 8200 www.netherlands.embassy.gov.au*

British Consulate – Koningslaan 44, 1075 AE Amsterdam, *31 (0)20 676 4343 http://ukinnl.fco.gov. uk/en*

Canadian Embassy – Sophialaan 7-2514 JP The Hague, *31 (0)70 311 1600 www.canada.nl*

Irish Embassy – Scheveningseweg 112, 2584AE Den Haag, *31 (0)70 363 0993 www.embassyofireland.nl*

United States Embassy – Lange Voorhout 102-2514 EJ The Hague, *31 (0)70 310 2209 http://thehague. usembassy.gov*

Entry Requirements

Nationals from a number of countries including the United States, Canada, Australia, New Zealand, the United Kingdom and Ireland need only a **valid passport** to enter the Netherlands for up to three months. European Union (EU) nationals entering the Netherlands need only their national identity card.

Nationals from other countries will need a Schengen visa, named after the Schengen Agreement, which ended internal border control between 25 European member countries. The Schengen visa is valid for up to 90 days; visitors wishing to stay longer will need to apply for a long-term visa known as an MVV. For a full explanation of entry and visa requirements and for a list of nationals who do and do not need a Schengen visa for the Netherlands, go to: *www.minbuza.nl*.

It is mandatory that you have personal identification on your person at all times during your stay in the Netherlands; failure to do so could result in a fine.

Customs

Visitors from EU countries can import, tax-free, the following: 110 liters beer; 90 liters wine; 20 liters fortified wine; 10 liters spirits; 800 cigarettes/400 cigars; 1 kilogram tobacco. Visitors from non-EU countries can import, tax-free, the following: 200 cigarettes/250 grams tobacco/50 cigars; 1 liter spirits; 2 liter fortified or sparkling wine; 50 grams perfume/0.25 liters eau de toilette; 500 grams coffee; 100 grams tea. **Prohibited items** include narcotics, firearms, ammunition and knives. For details

and a full list of prohibited items, access www.douane.nl/english. Cigars, cigarettes and alcohol above the designated amounts are among items brought into the Netherlands for which **duties** must be paid. Before you depart for the Netherlands, be sure to see the full list of prohibited and dutiable items online.

Health

Before You Go – There are no vaccinations required to enter the Netherlands. Residents of the EU and the UK should apply for a European Health Insurance Card (EHIC), which entitles the holder to free or reduced-cost medical care for accidents or unexpected illnesses while on vacation in EU countries. Visitors are strongly advised to take out additional travel insurance to cover against any expenses not covered by the EHIC, as well as lost luggage, theft, cancellation, delayed departure, etc. Non-EU travelers are advised to check with their insurance companies about taking out supplementary medical insurance with specific overseas coverage.

Health Services – Many hotels have a doctor on-call 24hrs a day. There are also several health services available to tourists: for the **tourist doctor** call *(020) 427 5011*. The Public Health Service in the Netherlands is the GGD; although the website is in Dutch (*www.ggd.nl*), communication by telephone can be made in English: *(020) 555 5911* (in Amsterdam); note that on weekends, this number is forwarded to the ambulance service (nonemergency).

Ambulance – Dial **112** for an ambulance.

Schiphol Airport Library ©Marieke van der Velden/NBTC

Hospitals – Below are two of the hospitals in which English is spoken:

- **OLVG (Onze Lieve Vrouwe Gasthuis)** – Oosterpark 9, *(020) 599 9111. www.olvg.nl*
- **VU Medisch Centrum** De Boelelaan 1117, *(020) 444 4444; www.vumc.com*

Pets – For cats and dogs, a general health certificate and proof of rabies vaccination should be obtained from your local veterinarian before departure.

GETTING THERE
By Air

Amsterdam Airport Schiphol - 0900 0141 *(0900 is a paid information number at a rate of €0.40 per minute)* from inside the Netherlands or (31) (0)20 794 0800 from outside the Netherlands. www.schiphol.com. Amsterdam's Schiphol Airport is the primary international airport of the Netherlands. It is an easy 15min train ride from Amsterdam's city center. One of the most efficient airports in Europe, Schiphol connects to several major destinations both within Europe and internationally.

After immigration and customs, passengers will enter a large plaza with information desks, ATMs and currency exchange booths, as well as trains, taxis, shuttles and buses to city center. Schipol has a library and, in the Schengen departures area, even an indoor/outdoor park, with a juice bar, exericise bikes with USB hookups, and bean bag chairs.

Airlines

A number of airlines serve Amsterdam from major international cities. Listed below are several of them:

- **British Airways** Schiphol Amsterdam Airport, Departure Hall 3, *020 346 9559. www.ba.com*
- **Cathay Pacific** Schiphol Amsterdam Airport, Departure Hall 3, *020 653 2010. www.cathaypacific.com*
- **Delta Air Lines** Schiphol Amsterdam Airport, Departure Hall 2, *020 721 9128. www.delta.com*
- **easyJet** Schiphol Amsterdam Airport, Departure Hall 3, *020 794 0800. www.easyjet.com*

- **KLM** – Schiphol Amsterdam Airport, Departure Hall 2, *020 474 7747. www.klm.com*
- **Transavia.com** – Schiphol Amsterdam Airport, Departure Hall 1, *0900 0737. www.transavia.com*

Airport Transfers

- **Bus – Connexxion** – *0900 266 6399, www.connexxion.nl*
Runs frequent service from Schiphol to Leidseplein in the city center. The bus takes about 30min and costs €10 for a return trip. Take bus route 197. Buses leave 5am–12am every 15min.
- **Shuttle Bus - Connexxion Schiphol Hotel Shuttle** *038 339 4741, www.airportotelshuttle.nl*
A shuttle service between more than 100 hotels and the airport. Services cost €15.50 one-way or €25.00 return. Buses leave 6am–9pm every 30min.
Tickets can be bought from your hotel or at the Connexxion desk at Schiphol. For more information, including a list of participating hotels, visit the website.
Taxi – Metered taxis wait outside the airport terminal. Taxis in Amsterdam are costly; expect to pay €45-55 to reach the city center. **Schiphol Travel Taxi** offers both private and shared taxi travel; for more details, visit *www.schiphol.com*
Train – The fastest and most convenient way to get to city center is by train. Located directly below Schiphol Airport, trains run roughly every 10min for the 15min ride to city center. Tickets can be purchased from the yellow ticket machines in the airport's plaza: €3.70 one-way.
For more information and timetables, visit *www.ns.nl/en*.

By Ship

- **DFDS Seaways** – *0871 522 9955, www.dfdsseaways.co.uk,* Operates a daily overnight service between Newcastle (England) and Ijmuiden (Amsterdam). From Ijmuiden you can easily reach Amsterdam by car, or by bus provided by DFDS Seaways; tickets can be purchased when booking the overnight ferry Fast Flying Ferry (*0900 266 6399, www. connexxion.nl*).

Hispeed train

©Mats Stafseng Einarsen/Michelin

By Train

Amsterdam's Centraal Station has regular train connections to and from Germany, Brussels, France and the UK.

♦ **From London** – Eurostar runs direct high-speed passenger trains from London to Brussels in less than 2hrs: *0843 218 6186; www.eurostar.com*.

From Brussels it is possible to take one of the frequent intercity trains to Amsterdam. In the UK, Rail Europe will make reservations for train trips between Brussels and the Netherlands: *0844 848 4064, www.raileuroper.co.uk*.

International **intercity journeys** are operated by **NS Hispeed**. It is advisable to book early for the best rates. Check the website below for more information about destinations, prices and timetables.

♦ **NS Hispeed** – *0900 9296. www.nshispeed.nl*

By Bus/Coach

Eurolines operates bus/coach service to Amsterdam from hundreds of destinations across Europe. To book and check schedules, view the website.

Eurolines

♦ **Rokin 10** – *088 076 1700. www.eurolines.com*.

By Car

The ring road A10, which circles the city, makes arriving and departing by car relatively easy. However, driving and parking in Amsterdam are difficult and expensive and may not be worth the hassle, especially since the city has an extensive and efficient public transport system *(see Getting Around below)*.

Road Regulations – Traffic in the Netherlands travels on the right. The minimum age for driving is 18 years for cars and motorcycles and 16 years for mopeds. Children under 12 are not allowed to travel in the front seat as long as there is room for them in the back.

Seatbelts are compulsory in the back as well as the front of the car. Maximum **speed limits** for cars, caravans and small trailers are 50kph/30mph in built-up areas, 80kph/50mph on the open road, and 120kph/75mph on motorways. Nationals of the European Union require a valid **national driving license**. Many nationals of non-EU countries such as the US, Australia and New Zealand can drive with a valid license for up to 180 days.

Parking – If you are arriving by car, your best option for parking is **P+R (Park & Ride)**. P+R spaces are located on the outskirts of Amsterdam in areas connecting them to the city center by frequent public transportation service. Parking costs €8.00 for 24hrs and includes public transportation to the city center for up to 5 people.

Gasoline – There are several **gas stations** around Amsterdam, but none witin the canal belt. Here are two stations that are close to the canal belt: Texaco on Marnixstraat 250 and Texaco on Sarphatistraat 225. Gas stations can also be found along highways. Foreign debit cards are not always accepted, so it's best to carry a credit card or cash. Gas is sold by the **liter**.

In Case of Accident – If you are involved in an accident and require emergency assistance, dial **112** for the police/ambulance. For 24-hour roadside assistance, contact the **ANWB** (the Royal Dutch

PRACTICAL INFORMATION

Bicycles and cyclists

©Mats Stafseng Einarsen/Michelin

Touring Club), a Dutch automobile association, at **088 269 2888**.

Car Rental – Cars can be rented at Schiphol airport and in several areas around city center if you have a valid driver's license; the minimum age to rent a car is 21 years. Telephone numbers for rental offices at the airport are.

Rental Car Companies

Avis

- Schiphol Arrivals Hall, *020 655 6050. www.avis.com*

Europcar

- Overtoom 197, *020 683 2123. www.europcar.com*

Hertz

- Schiphol Arrivals Hall 3, *020 502 0240*
- Overtoom 333, *020 612 2441. www.hertz.com*

GETTING AROUND
By Bicycle

With its flat terrain, extensive bike paths and narrow streets that don't accommodate cars, Amsterdam is ideal for cycling. There is no better way to get around.

Bicycle Rental – Some hotels have bikes available but only for overnight guests. Here are a few of the companies around Amsterdam that offer bicycle rental.

AmsterBike (*www.amsterbike.eu*) near the Passenger Terminal east of Centraal Station at Piet Heinkade 11, 020 419 9063.

Fietsreparatie Amsterdam (*www. fietsreparatieamsterdam.nl*) in north Amsterdam at Meerpad 2, 061 399 8675.

MacBike (*€9.50 per day, www. macbike.nl*) at Weteringschans 2, 020 528 7688; Marnixstraat 220, 020 626 6964; Waterlooplein 199, 020 428 7005; and Stationsplein 5, 020 624 8391.

Orange Bike (*€9.50 per day, www.orangebike.nl*) at Singel 233, 020 528 9990; and Geldersekade 37, 020 779 4635.

Biking Safety Tips

- Stay in the bicycle lanes, marked by white lines and bike symbols.
- Do not cycle on footpaths, shopping streets or squares. Cyclists are not allowed on paths designed for pedestrians.
- Keep to the right, and pass other bicycles or mopeds on the left.
- Other traffic must be passed on the right. Put out your hand to signal a change of direction.
- Watch out for tram tracks and cross them at a sharp angle; bicycle wheels easily get stuck and lead to serious accidents.
- Make sure to lock your bike securely: bike theft is a major problem in Amsterdam.

MUST KNOW

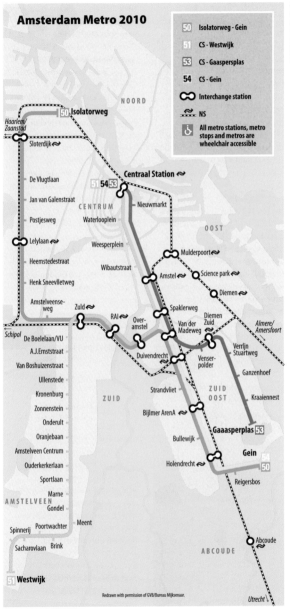

Amsterdam Metro 2010

50	Isolatorweg - Gein
51	CS - Westwijk
53	CS - Gaaspersplas
54	CS - Gein
🞤	Interchange station
≈	NS
♿	All metro stations, metro stops and metros are wheelchair accessible

Redrawn with permission of GVB/Bureau Mijksenaar.

By Public Transport

Amsterdam has an excellent public transportation system combining buses, trams and the metro run by the municipal transport company **GVB** (Gemeentelijk Vervoerbedrijf), with frequent service connecting to the major attractions. For more information, visit *www.gvb.nl/english*.

Tickets – OV Chipkaart are valid for rides on trams, buses and the metro throughout Amsterdam. They can be purchased at railway stations at Ticket Vending and Add Value Machines for a fee of €7.50 but you will need to add credit to the card once the initial amount is used. It is cheaper than buying a single ticket each time you travel by bus, tram or metro. Be sure to **scan the card** upon entry and exit and when changing vehicles (forgetting to scan the card on exit results in charges of the cost for the maximum distance).

Amsterdam's modern trams

GVB Tickets - On the tram you can buy a 1hr ticket for €2.60 or a 24hr ticket for €7.00. For information about times and routes, visit *www.journeyplanner.9292.nl*.

On Foot

Walking is an excellent way to take in Amsterdam's beauty and absorb its laid-back atmosphere. Because the city is so compact, almost everything in the historic center is easily accessible on foot within about 30min. But be alert for the city's many cyclists who dominate the streets and bridges.

ACCESSIBILITY

Many restaurants, museums and hotels in Amsterdam provide access for people with disabilities. For information about the accessibility of public buildings and public transport in Amsterdam, go online to *www.toegankelijkamsterdam.nl*.

Netherlands Railways offers a comprehensive service for the disabled traveler that includes a free escort service; call at least 3hrs ahead to reserve. Train timetables are available in Braille.

Most new trams are accessible for wheelchair-users as are raised platforms at tram stops, particularly lines 1,5, 13, 17 and 26.

All **metro stations** are accessible for wheelchair users. Folded wheelchairs will fit in most taxis, and there are also special taxi and minibus taxi services for disabled travelers.

It is advisable to book taxis in advance. Here is one company that is open 24hrs daily:

Taxi & Touringcar Lagerberg B.V. – 31 (0)20 647 4700.
www.taxi-lagerberg.nl

©Mats Stafseng Einarsen/Michelin

BASIC INFORMATION
Accommodations

For suggested lodgings, see Hotels at the back of the guide. The Amsterdam Tourism & Convention Board maintains an online **hotel directory** and reservations service. For more information, or to book a hotel, access *www.iamsterdam.com*.

Business Hours

Banks – Generally open Mon 10am–4pm or 5pm and Tue–Fri 9am–4pm or 5pm. However, opening times vary from one branch to another. Some banks stay open during late-night shopping on Thursdays.

Post Offices – Generally open Mon–Fri 8:30am–5pm and Sat 8:30am–noon.

Shops – Usually open Mon 10am–6pm, Tue–Fri 9am–6pm and Sat 10am–5pm; outside the main shopping areas, many are closed on Sun and Mon mornings (sometimes all day Monday). Thursday is a late shopping night; most shops stay open until 9pm. Supermarkets are open Mon–Fri 8am–8pm, Sat–Sun 8am–6pm.

GWK Travelex – Offices are open Mon–Sat 8am–8pm and Sun 10am–4pm. Longer opening hours from 8am–10pm can be found at Amsterdam Centraal Station and Leidseplein.

Pharmacies – Open Mon–Fri 9am–5:30pm and Sat 10am–5pm.

Discounts

An annual museum card, **Museumkaart**, allows entry to more than 400 museums all over the Netherlands at a cost of €39.95 for adults and €19.95 for children under 18. The card can be purchased at most affiliated museums or at the Uitburo in Leidseplein. For more information visit *www.museumkaart.nl*.

The **I amsterdam City Card** permits holders entry to selected museums, free transport on trains, buses and the metro, and discounts at selected restaurants and attractions. You can choose cards that are valid for a duration of 24hrs (€39), 48hrs (€49) and 72hrs (€59). For details, access *www.iamsterdam.com/en/visiting/iamsterdamcard/deiamsterdamcard*.

Electricity

Electrical current is supplied at 220 volts AC. Plugs are round two-pin so, if needed, bring a **universal** adapter to recharge your mobile phone or use other personal appliances. Most hotels should be able to provide an adapter.

Internet

Wireless Internet is widely available at Amsterdam's hotels as well as cafes, where you can access the Internet with your laptop or phone, often at no charge. A large number

Important Phone Numbers	
Emergency (police, ambulance, fire)	☎ **112**
Police	☎ 0900 8844
Tourist Doctor	☎ 020 427 5011
Roadside Assistance (ANWB)	☎ 088 269 2888

of Internet cafes are located throughout the city. Amsterdam's city library, Openbare Bibliotheken Amsterdam, offers free Wi-Fi; valid personal identification is required.

OBA - Openbare Bibliotheken Amsterdam – *Oosterdokskade 143, 020 523 0800*

Mail/Post

The country is closing its traditional post offices, but most major hotels offer postal, telephone, Internet and photocopying services. Shops offering postal services are identified with an orange PostNL or TNT poster on their window. Stamps can also be bought from shops selling postcards. Letters and postcards can be dropped into orange postal boxes that are found throughout the city. Rates to the US and Canada are €0.95 for first-class letters and postcards. Rates to the UK are €0.79 for first-class letters and postcards.

Money

Currency – The unit of currency in the Netherlands is the European **euro** (€) comprising 100 cents. Coins come in denominations of €0.01, €0.02, €0.05, €0.10, €0.20, €0.50 cents, and €1 and €2 euros. Banknote denominations are 5€, 10€, 20€, 50€, 100€, 200€, and 500€ euros. Note that 200€ and 500€ banknotes are not common and are not accepted by most businesses. At the time of publication, 1 EUR was equivalent to 1.44 USD Dollar, 1.30 AUD Dollar and .88 GBP (British Pound).

Currency Exchange – Traveler's checks can be exchanged at banks and some major exchange offices. Foreign cash can be exchanged at post offices, banks and exchange offices. Rates of commission vary among exchange bureaus, so check before changing your money. For up-to-date **exchange rates**, access *www.xe.com*.

GWK Travelex offices are found throughout the city. They are usually open Mon–Sun early morning to late at night. Most GWK offices also offer a hotel booking service, tickets to major attractions, maps and tourist guides.

Credit Cards – International credit cards (American Express, Diners Club, Eurocard, Visa, Access and MasterCard) are accepted in most shops, hotels and restaurants, but not in all; it is advisable to ask ahead of time and have enough cash to cover your bill. Some shops might add a 5 percent charge for credit card payments.

ATMs – Visitors can also obtain cash from ATM bank machines outside most banks, train stations and shops that accept credit and debit cards.

Public Holidays

1 January
Good Friday
Easter Sunday and **Monday**
30 April (Queen's Day or National Day)
Ascension Day
Whit Sunday
Whit Monday
5 May (Liberation Day)
25 and **26 December**
Local festivals *(see Calendar of Events)* can also mean that various public facilities will be closed.

Smoking

Since July 2008, a smoking ban has been in force in the Dutch hospitality industry, with the exception of special "smoking rooms" in some bars, cafes and restaurants; most restaurants do not have a smoking room. Because smoking rooms are not designated exclusively for smokers, other activities, like drinking, eating and dancing are allowed. Smoking is also permitted on terraces.

Telephones

To phone abroad from the Netherlands, dial the international access code as follows:

UK: 00 44
Australia: 00 61
US/Canada: 00 1
Ireland: 00 353

followed by the area code (without the first '0') and the 7-digit number. The country code for the Netherlands is 31. The area code for Amsterdam is 020.

When calling the Netherlands from the US, dial the international access code 011 followed by 31 country code for the Netherlands, then the city area code and 7-digit number. To call Amsterdam from abroad, dial 011 + 31+20 plus the 7-digit phone number in Amsterdam.

To call within the Netherlands, dial the city's area code plus the 7-digit number. To call within Amsterdam, dial only the 7-digit number. It is not necessary to dial the area code. Telephone numbers beginning with 0800 are toll-free. Those beginning with 0900 are charged at premium rate calls (€0.40 per minute). Those beginning 0600 are mobile phone numbers.

Public **telephone booths** in Amsterdam are green and credit-card operated. Many booths still accept coins and phone cards; phone cards are available from bookshops, news agents, tourist offices and tobacco stores.

Amsterdam phone booth
©Mats Stafseng Einarsen/Michelin

Time

The Netherlands is on Central European Time (Greenwich Mean Time + 1hr, EST -6hrs).

Taxes

The Netherlands has a **Value Added Tax (VAT)**. The tax is 6 percent on food, on basic items and on hotel accommodations, and 19 percent on beverages, on clothes and on luxury items. In restaurants VAT is included in the prices on the menu. In shops, VAT is included on the price tag. Restaurants add a 5 percent service charge, which is included in the menu price. In hotels, the room rate includes the VAT and a service charge, but there is also a city tax that is 5 percent of the room rate.

Tipping

For hotels, restaurants, shopping and taxis, the bill is usually inclusive of service charge and VAT. However a 5-10 percent tip or rounding up of the bill is always appreciated.

33

VENICE OF THE NORTH

Somewhat centrally located in the northern part of the Netherlands, Amsterdam★★★ lies on the banks of two rivers, the IJ and the Amstel. Built on water like Venice—its great rival in days gone by—Amsterdam sits about 20km/12mi inland east of the North Sea, at the southern end of a large freshwater lake, the IJsselmeer. Its geographical location has help forged its position as an important international port and one of Europe's most dynamic cities. While The Hague is the seat of the nation's government, Amsterdam serves as its capital. As the largest city in the Netherlands, Amsterdam is home to some 770,000 people, many of whom live along its 165 canals.

The first documented mention of the city dates from 1275, when Count Floris V of Holland granted toll privileges to this **herring-fishing village**, situated on two dikes joined by a dam at the mouth of the Amstel River. Amsterdam developed in stages around the original village center, present-day Dam square. It was awarded its city charter in about 1300, and was annexed by William III to the county of Holland in 1317. A period of great affluence began in the late 16C. After Antwerp had been pillaged by the Spanish in 1576, the town's rich merchants took refuge in Amsterdam, bringing their **diamond industry** with them. Once Amsterdam had

Amsterdam Fast Facts

- **Area:** 322sq km/124sq mi
- **City population:** 770,000
- **Annual visitors:** 5.3 million
- **Year of independence:** 1648
- **Form of government:** Mayor, aldermen and municipal council
- **Airlines servicing Schipol:** 89
- **Amsterdam's port:** 49 million tons unloaded, 24 million loaded (2010)

been freed from Spanish rule by the Union of Utrecht in 1579, the town became very prosperous, not least because of the large-scale influx of immigrants. The famous painter **Rembrandt**, who was born in Leiden, came to live in Amsterdam in 1630, and was buried in the Westerkerk in 1669. The 17C, the city's **Golden Age,** marked the height of Amsterdam's powers. Seventeenth-century Europe had only two truly independent cities, Venice and Amsterdam. Each of these powerful, rival cities was the capital of a republic. Venice had a Roman Catholic aristocratic elite; Amsterdam was headed by a Protestant upper middle class. In the wake of the Portuguese, the Dutch had gone **exploring**: Cornelius de Houtman landed in Java, Indonesia, in 1596. Jacob van Neck conquered the island of Mauritius in 1598. Australia was first mapped by Dutch cartographers, who called it Nieuw-Holland.

By the 17C Dutch sailing ships were trading all over the Far East. In 1602 they founded the **East India Company** to coordinate the large number of trading companies sailing to the East; it

Reclaiming the Land

The sea is a constant threat: more than a third of the Netherlands lies below sea level (Amsterdam sits only 6.5ft above sea level). The name Netherlands comes from the Dutch words for "low"(neder) and "country" (land). Without protection from dunes and dikes, more than half the country would be under water during surge tides or river risings.

The large freshwater lake northeast of Amsterdam, the IJsselmeer, was first a vast arm of the North Sea called the Zuiderzee, created in 1287 when there were at least 35 great floods. In the 14C windmills were being used to drain the land. As early as 1667 the draining of the Zuiderzee was proposed, to be rid of the violent North Sea waters. But it was not until 1932 that the Zuiderzee Project closed off the sea by a barrier dam, and created the IJsselmeer. Once enclosed, work began on draining several polders around the edge. A polder is land reclaimed from the sea, a lake or marshland. The area is enclosed with dikes and then pumping begins to regulate the water level, the same method used since the earliest of times.

soon became the largest trading company of the 17C. Dutch trade turned toward the New World. The first expedition was that of **Henry Hudson** in 1609, who crossed the Atlantic into what was later named Hudson's Bay. Java became a Dutch colony in 1619. In 1621 the West India Company was founded. Jan Anthoniszoon van Riebeeck established the Cape Colony (South Africa) in 1652. A Dutch settlement was established at **Nieuw Amsterdam**, later renamed New York by the British. The growth of navigation led to an increased demand for maps and globes, and their manufacture became one of Amsterdam's specialities. The city acquired a leading reputation in this area, partly as a result of the work of famous cartographers such as Hondius, who published a new edition of Mercator's famous atlas in 1605.

©Michael Maslan Historic Photographs/Corbis

Amsterdam, 1880s-1890s

The Wisselbank, created in 1609, was one of Europe's first banks, and Amsterdam's Stock Exchange was built in 1608 by Hendrick de Keyser. In 1610 it was decided to build Amsterdam's three **main canals**, the Herengracht, Keizersgracht and Prinsengracht; soon they were lined with the mansions of wealthy merchants. The horseshoe shape core of the city was surrounded by a high wall on which a number of **windmills** were built.

Such was Amsterdam's accumulated wealth that for a long time it withstood the effects of the economic decline of the 18C. In 1672 the city had contrived to repel an attack by Louis XIV's troops by opening the locks that protected it, but it could do nothing in 1795 against France's army under the command of Charles Pichegru. In 1806 **Napoleon** made his brother Louis Bonaparte king of Holland. Louis settled in Amsterdam, which became the capital of the kingdom. The country became a part of France in 1810. However,

Amsterdam was seriously hit by Napoleon's blockade of Britain, the Continental System, which ruined its trade. In November 1813 the population revolted and recognized the prince of Orange, William I, as their sovereign on 2 December 1813.

It was only in the second half of the 19C that the city emerged from a long period of economic lethargy. The city walls were demolished and the opening of the Noordzeekanaal in 1876 provided a major boost to overseas trade. In 1889 the Centraal Station was built in Amsterdam. The diamond industry also began to flourish again.

In 1903 the new Stock Exchange by **Berlage** was completed, marking the beginning of a new era of architecture. Shortly before World War I, the city began expanding and new suburbs were built. The **Amsterdam School** of architecture developed a new style of building, mainly after World War I, and designed a great deal of local authority housing, particularly to the south of

Amsterdam today

©NBTC

Sarphatipark and to the west of **Spaarndammerstraat**.

World War II hit the city badly. Under the five-year German occupation, nearly 80,000 Jews were deported to concentration camps; only 5,000 survived. After the war, Amsterdam gradually staged a magnificent recovery. It is now a major industrial city, part of the huge, crescent-shaped **Randstad conurbation** that includes Utrecht and Rotterdam. Its industries encompass medical technology, metals, printing, food, and tourism. The **RAI**, built on Europaplein in the 1960s, hosts many international congresses and trade fairs, and the **World Trade Center** near Zuid Station was opened in 1985.

The 72km/45mi canal from Amsterdam to the Rhine River (Amsterdam-Rijnkanaal), finished in 1952, has contributed to the development of the port. The completion of a road tunnel under the IJ in 1968 improved interaction between the city center and the area north of the port. The first metro line began service in 1976. The city has seen the growth of such modern suburbs as **Buitenveldert** to the south and **Bijlmermeer** to the southeast. However, the housing problem remains acute, and the city continues to expand, as seen in some 2,400 picturesque houseboats lining 36km/22mi of quays. Amsterdam has two universities and numerous higher educational institutions. The lack of tall buildings and wide roads gives Amsterdam a small-town atmosphere. Another of its most striking features is the dominance of the bicycle as a means of transport; it is said that Amsterdam has nearly as many bicycles as it does residents.

Amsterdam is home to some of Europe's most famous attractions, world-class museums, celebrated architecture, and a thriving cafe society. Its great cultural wealth includes the major exhibitions of the **Rijksmuseum**, the **Van Gogh Museum** and the **Stedelijk Museum**, numerous art galleries in and around Nieuwe Spiegelstraat, concerts by the world-famous Concertgebouw Orchestra, the Holland Festival, the Prinsengrachtfestival outside the Pulitzer hotel in summer, and the Uitmarkt, heralding the beginning of the new theater season.

The city has some of the best nightlife in the world: cozy "brown cafes," trendy alternative bars, discos, nightclubs and of course the infamous red-light district, the **Walletjes**. Amsterdam is a very outward-looking and tolerant city. As elsewhere in the Netherlands, many Amsterdam coffee shops sell soft drugs legally.

Progressive, libertarian and unconventional in many respects, the city continues to evolve as a model of first-class transit (a new **North-South metro line** will stretch from Centraal Station to the south station by 2017). It remains an educational and cultural trailblazer as well: witness the new central library, the new music **conservatory** of the Amsterdam School of the Arts and ongoing upgrades of the Rijksmuseum, the Van Gogh Museum and the Stedelijk Museum. The latter's "bathtub" design for its new facade is among groundbreaking trends in architecture.

DISTRICTS

Although Amsterdam is experiencing growth in new redevelopment zones outside the historic core, its architectural and cultural heritage is preserved in Old Amsterdam and adjacent neighborhoods. From the landmark central train station edging the Het IJ (the IJ River), Amsterdam spreads out in a concentric half web of canal-lined streets packed with public squares and fanciful buildings. Eminently walkable, the compact city center can be covered in one day, but it's best to allow several days to savor side streets, stop at a cafe and leisurely stroll along a canal in addition to visiting specific attractions. Must Sees that should not be missed are Old Amsterdam, The Canals, the Port, the Pijp, and the Museum Quarter *(see Old Masters)*.

OLD AMSTERDAM★★★

The "new side" or **Nieuwe Zijde**, together with the "old side," the **Oude Zijde**, form the heart of Old Amsterdam. Both as old as the city itself, the sides were given their names for reasons relating to parish boundaries.

The main square, called simply the **Dam★**, sits on the site of the dam across the Amstel River. It's a useful dividing line between the old and new sections of the city, located, as it is, at the junction of the two central thoroughfares, the **Damrak** and the Rokin. Nieuwe Zijde, west of Damrak, was historically the parish of the Dam's majestic Nieuwe Kerk, which shares the square with the **Royal Palace**, one of Queen Beatrix's trio of palaces. Nearby Kalverstraat intersperses affordable fashion with favorite attractions like the Amsterdam Museum, while cross street Het Spui culminates in a square full of cafe terraces, markets and bookstores. East of Damrak, the Oude Zijde was the domain of the 14C **Oude Kerk**, located on a

Interior, Royal Palace

©ATCB

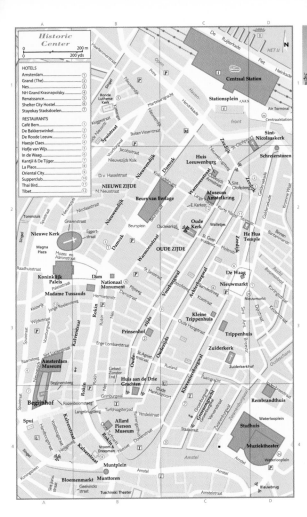

Historic Center

0   200 m
0   200 yds

HOTELS
Amsterdam .... ①
Grand (The) .... ②
Nes .... ③
NH Grand Krasnapolsky .... ④
Renaissance .... ⑤
Shelter City Hostel .... ⑥
Stayokay Stadsdoelen .... ⑦

RESTAURANTS
Café Bern .... ①
De Bakkerswinkel .... ②
De Roode Leeuw .... ③
Haesje Claes .... ④
Hofje van Wijs .... ⑤
In de Waag .... ⑥
Kantjil & De Tijger .... ⑦
La Place .... ⑧
Oriental City .... ⑨
Supperclub .... ⑩
Thai Bird .... ⑪
Tibet .... ⑫

---

placid square in the heart of
De Walletjes, the red-light
district. This side of the old city
center takes in Amsterdam's
Chinatown, the cafes and coffee
shops of Nieuwmarkt square, and
the Jodenbuurt, the former
Jewish quarter with five
synagogues.

Nieuwe Zijde★★
The Big Three

Centraal Station
*Stationsplein, at the northeast
end of city center, on the edge of
the IJ River. Open 24hrs.*
The imposing main train station
occupies three artificial islands in

Piled High

Because much of Amsterdam is built on reclaimed marshland, the buildings needed to be well grounded. Amsterdam's churches, canal houses and the royal palace were erected using thousands of freestanding wooden piles, called *heipalen*, as supports. They were sunk deep into firm ground usually some 13m/42ft or so below the surface level, where layers of sand and clay alter with layers of peat or sand and layers of a mixture of sand and peat.

the IJ River. The building caused great controversy when it was completed in 1889, mainly because it blocked off the view of the port. Designed by architects P.J.H. Cuypers and A.L. van Gendt, it is now one of the city's best-known structures *(see Architecture)*.

Nieuwe Kerk★★

Dam square. Open daily 10am–5pm. Closed 25 Dec & 1 Jan. €5, children15 and under free. 020 638 6909.www.nieuwekerk.nl.
The Protestant New Church is the national church of the Netherlands, where the country's sovereigns are crowned. Catholic mass was first held here in 1410; but after the Reformation, the services were

Protestant. This Late Gothic edifice was pillaged and gutted by fire several times. After the fire in 1645, its tower remained unfinished. Now an exhibition venue, the building is used as a cultural center, where all kinds of activities are organized.

Koninklijk Paleis★

Open daily noon–5pm (Jul–Aug 11am–5pm). €7.50, children 5-16 €6.50, under 5 free. 020 620 4060. www.paleisamsterdam.nl.
The town hall became the Royal Palace in 1808, during the reign of Louis Bonaparte. This monumental Classical-style building was built on 13,659 wooden piles.
Located on the ground floor is the **Vierschaar**, the courtroom where death sentences used to be passed. The public could watch the proceedings through the grilles.

History Capsules

Amsterdam Museum★★

Access via Kalverstraat 92, Nieuwezijds Voorburgwal 357 or Sint Luciënsteeg 27. Open Mon–Fri 10am–5pm, Sat–Sun and public holidays 11am–5pm. Closed 1 Jan, 30 Apr and 25 Dec. €10, children 6-18 €5, under 6 free. 020 523 1822. www.amsterdammuseum.nl.
This museum *(see Museums)* is housed in a 15C former orphanage.

Centraal Station

©Kristen de Joseph/Michelin

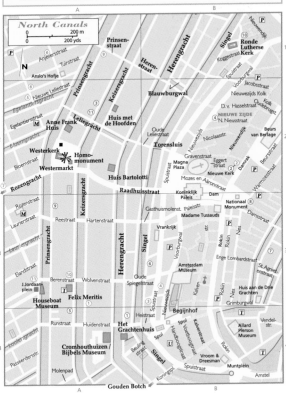

On the left of the entrance in Kalverstraat lies the boys' playground. Opposite, a building in the Classical style hosts temporary exhibits. The entrance to the museum is through the second courtyard, formerly reserved for the female orphans.

Begijnhof★★

Founded in the 14C, the Beguine convent is one of the few such institutions remaining in the Netherlands. Beguines are women belonging to a lay sisterhood; although they take no vows, they devote themselves to religious

41

DISTRICTS

Façade Stones

After the huge fire of 1452, all new houses were required to be built of stone with tile roofs. In the absence of house numbers, a small sculpted **façade** stone was used, showing the emblem of the owner or the symbol of his trade. This practice ended when house numbering was introduced by the French. Such **façade**, or gable, stones are still sometimes used today.

life and wear a habit.

The tall 17C and 18C houses with small front gardens are arranged around an area of grass where the former church of the Beguines stands. This complex has belonged to the English Presbyterian community since 1607. Note that nos. 11, 19, 23 and 24 have sculpted **façade stones**.

The tall house at no. 26 was that of the mother superior of the Beguinage. At no. 29 there is a hidden Catholic chapel, built by the Beguines in 1665.

Madame Tussauds

Dam 20. Open daily 10am–6:30pm (Jul–Aug 10am–8:30pm). Closed 30 Apr. €21, children 5-15 €16, under 5 free. 020 522 1010. www.madametussauds.nl.

Here modern technology, including audio-animatronics, is used to create a fascinating museum illustrating mainly life during Amsterdam's Golden Age (the 1600s), as depicted in the paintings of Rembrandt, Vermeer and Jan Steen. Don't miss the **revolving model** of 17C Amsterdam. The exhibit ends with many well-known figures from the Netherlands and abroad.

Begijnhof

Oude Zijde★★
Houses of Worship

Oude Kerk★

Oudekerksplein. Open Mon–Sat
11am–5pm, Sun 1pm–5pm.
Closed 1 Jan, 30 Apr, 25 Dec.
€5, children under 13 free
(additional €5 to visit the tower;
tours Sat & Sun 1pm–5pm on the
half hour). 020 625 8284.
www.oudekerk.nl.

Dedicated to St. Nicholas, the
present Old Church was built in
1306, the oldest in the city. In the
16C the bell tower was topped by
an elegant spire whose carillon
was in part cast by François
Hemony; there is an excellent
view★★ from here.

The Lady Chapel has three
stained-glass windows★ (1555).
The **organ loft★** (1724) was
the work of Jan Westerman.
Rembrandt's wife was buried
here in 1642. The church is
the final resting place of many
famous people, including painter
Pieter Aertsen, writer Roemer
Visscher, architects Justus and
Philips Vingboons and composer
JP Sweelinck. The church hosts
organ recitals, exhibits, theater
performances and other events.

Organ loft, Oude Kerk

© P. Gajic/MICHELIN

Museum Amstelkring★

Oudezijds Voorburgwal 40. Open
Mon–Sat 10am–5pm, Sun and
public holidays 1pm–5pm. Closed
1 Jan and 30 Apr. €8, children 6–18
€4, under 6 free. 020 624 6604.
www.opsolder.nl.

This museum is also known as
Museum Ons' Lieve Heer op
Solder. After the Union of Utrecht
in 1579, when the Catholics were
driven out of their churches by the
Reformation, they were forced to
celebrate mass in private houses.
Although such worship was
officially prohibited, in practice

Best Views in Town

Amsterdam's best views are obtainable at obvious and not-so-obvious
places. The distinctive rooftop terrace of Science Center **NEMO** *(see For*
Kids) offers an outdoor perch from which to admire the skyline *(Jun–Sept*
daily noon–7pm); the **Westerkerk** clock tower, the tallest church tower in
Amsterdam, rewards visitors who ascend its 85m//280ft with panoramic
views *(tours Apr–Oct; €7; 020 689 2565; for information, email anna@buscher-*
malocca.nl). Other opportunities to take in the cityscape from atop a
monumental church tower are available at the **Zuiderkerk** *(Apr–Sept 1pm–*
5pm; €6) and the **Oude Kerk** *(tours Sat & Sun 1pm–5pm on the half hour; €5;*
020 625 8284; www.oudekerk.nl).

DISTRICTS

Hall, Museum Amstelkring

©P. Gajic/MICHELIN

the authorities turned a blind eye. This secret chapel in the attics of two houses was used for Catholic worship from 1663 until the construction of the new **Sint Nicolaaskerk** in 1887.

The staircase leading to the second floor passes in front of the hall, which is in pure 17C Amsterdam style. Take a look at the box bed in the curate's room. The **church**, whose two superimposed galleries occupy the third and fourth floors of the houses, has 18C furnishings.

Zuiderkerk

Zuiderkerkhof 72. Open Mon–Fri 10am–5pm, Sat by appointment. 088 020 2208. www.zuiderkerk. innl.nl.

The Zuiderkerk (Southern Church), completed in 1611, was the first church in Amsterdam built especially for Protestant services. Architect Hendrick de Keyser rendered the church in his trademark Amsterdam Renaissance style, familiar from other historic Amsterdam churches such as the Westerkerk and Noorderkerk. De

Keyser himself is buried in the church, as is Rembrandt's most illustrious pupil, Ferdinand Bol, and three of Rembrandt's children. Claude Monet featured the church in a characteristically impressionist cityscape that he painted during an 1874 visit to Amsterdam.

Universiteitsmuseum de Agnietenkapel
Oudezijds Voorburgwal 231.

The **Agnietenpoort** leads to this chapel, once the home of the Athenaeum Illustre of 1632, a predecessor of the university. The buildings are currently being used by the university, and temporary exhibitions are held here.

Houses of Ill Repute

The Walletjes★★
Bounded by Warmoesstraat, Damstraat, Oude Doelenstraat, Kloveniersburgwal, Nieuwmarkt and Geldersekade.

Amsterdam's famous **red-light district** is sometimes called "Walletjes" by the locals. It was once frequented by seafarers from the 14C onwards. The word means "small walls" and refers to the fact that the shop windows lit with pinkish-red neon lights in which prostitutes pose are sometimes half-concealed in old, narrow streets (particularly to the south of Oude Kerk). Today the industry has become much less light-hearted, with sex shops and stores selling pornographic videos. The area is not dangerous—indeed avoiding it would mean missing out on a large section of the historic center—but be on guard because the area is well known for pickpockets.

⚜ Historic Houses

Huis Leeuwenburg
Oudezijds Voorburgwal 14.
This picturesque 17C house has a stepped gable of rust-colored brick. A carved façade stone shows a castle sheltering a lion.
From the bridge over the lock where the two canals meet, an attractive **view★** reveals the Oudezijds Kolk and the dome of Sint Nicolaaskerk on one side, the **Oudezijds Voorburgwal★** with its old façades on the other side.

Trippenhuis
Kloveniersburgwal 29.
This classical edifice was built in 1662 by Justus Vingboons for the Trip brothers, who were cannon manufacturers; the chimneys are in the shape of mortars. As the widest canal house in Amsterdam, it stands in stark contrast to the small picturesque house across the canal at **no. 26**, called the **Kleine Trippenhuis** (Small Trip House). In popular lore, the Trips' coachman wished for a house merely as wide as the front door of the Trippenhuis; the Trips used stone left over from the main house to grant his wish.
The Klein Trippenhuis was constructed only after the Trip brothers' death.

Huis aan de Drie Grachten★
This "House on the Three Canals," dating from 1609, stands at the confluence of the Oudezijds Voorburgwal, the Oudezijds Achterburgwal, and the Grimburgwal. The Grimburgwal Canal was built in the early 14C and marked the southern boundary of the city.

Chinatown and Nieuwmarkt

Amsterdam's Chinatown is more compact than its international counterparts, but has the familiar emphasis on food, traditional skills and trinket sellers. Historically, it was concentrated along Binnen Bantammerstraat, where a Chinese community sprouted up around 1900; since then, it has spread outwards to nearby streets, each of which has a Dutch and a Chinese street name. The **Zeedijk** is a conduit from the train station area to the open sprawl of Nieuwmarkt square, which on sunny days is lined with cafe terraces. What pulls in the crowds are Chinatown's cosmopolitan eateries: not only is much of Asia represented on its restaurant menus, but also an excellent cross-section of Dutch specialties in its bakeries, cafes and delicatessens.
Amsterdam's oldest market square, **Nieuwmarkt** (New Market) is a favorite spot to idle at a terraced cafe, restaurant or coffee shop. True to its name, Nieuwmarkt is the site of a **daily market**.

The Walletjes, red-light district

© Bjørn Svensson / age fotostock

Zeedijk 1
Zeedijk 1.
One of only two wooden houses that survive south of the IJ River, this one was built in the mid-16C. Most of its streets in Chinatown are lined with typical row houses whose quaint façades conceal a sturdiness that, in some cases, has lasted since the 16C.

🚶 He Hua Temple
Zeedijk 106-118. Open Mon–Sat noon–5pm, Sun 10am–5pm; 020 420 2357; www.ibps.nl.
This Buddhist temple stands out above the dense thicket of restaurants and storefronts. Beyond its typical monastery entrance, visitors can take a half-hour tour *(Sat 3pm, 4pm and 5pm; €5)* and even cap it off with an optional meditation session *(€3)*.

De Waag
Nieuwmarkt Square.
An example of vernacular Gothic architecture, the public weights and measures office has survived since its construction in the late 15C. Once called the Sint Antoniespoort (St. Anthony's Gate), it comprised part of the medieval city walls until they were demolished in the 17C. (Another remnant of these walls, the Schreierstoren, can be found on the Prins Hendrikkade.) Today a fortified gateway flanked by towers and turrets with pepperpot roofs remains.

From 1617, De Waag assumed the function for which it's named: a weighing house where taxes were levied on merchandise, which was then sold on the square or transported elsewhere. Also situated in one of the towers was the anatomical theater, where public dissections—such as the one depicted in Rembrandt's famous *Anatomy Lesson of Dr. Nicholas Tulp*, now in The Hague's Mauritshuis—were held annually. Since 1996, the renovated space has harbored restaurant-cafe **In De Waag** *(see Restaurants)*, whose classic, candle-lit interior complements its historic backdrop.

Plein and Fancy
Explore a number of Amsterdam's public squares or "pleins." Begin at the city's famed flower market.

Bloemenmarkt★★
Located at the southern end of the Singel canal, this colorful flower market, filled with an array of fanciful blooms, has been in existence since 1862. It offers passers-by a wide selection of cut flowers and bulbs as well as clogs and other souvenirs *(see Shopping)*.

Muntplein
East of the flower market, this busy square *(plein)* is dominated by the Mint Tower, **Munttoren**. The tower,

He Hua Temple

©Kristen de Joseph/Michelin

MUST SEE

Rembrandtplein

the remains of a 17C gateway, has a Baroque spire added by Hendrick de Keyser and a **carillon**. In 1672, during the war against France, money was minted here.

Rembrandtplein★

This square is a popular destination for local people out for an evening stroll. Many large cafes surround the square, with its statue of **Rembrandt** by Royer (1852). About equidistant from the Muntplein and Rembrandtplein sits the **Pathé Tuschinski** *(Reguliersbreestraat 26-34; 0900 1458; www.pathe.nl/bioscoop/ tuschinski)*. This cinema was built in 1921 by HL de Jong, and combines Art-Deco and Art Noveau styles with elements from the Amsterdam School of architecture. Note the expressive **façade**, and as you enter, the handsome carpet in the foyer. The **interior★** of the Tuschinski 1 auditorium is remarkable for its ornamented ceiling and proscenium arch. Opposite, the building that was once the Cineac cinema (1934, J Duiker) still retains the spirit

of its former inhabitant. The exterior is a good example of the differences between Art Deco and Functionalism.

Thorbeckeplein

With its many nightclubs, this square is very busy in the evenings *(see Nightlife)*.

Waterlooplein

On this large square, which has a lively **daily market** *(see Shopping)*, stands the **Mozes-en Aäron Kerk**, a Catholic church (1841) now used for exhibitions and concerts. The southern part of the square is occupied by the highly controversial **Stopera** (1987) (from *stadhuis* and *opera*). Residents in the vicinity feared that its contemporary form would be a blight on the historic city center. The modern complex includes the **Muziektheater** *(see Performing Arts)* and the **Stadhuis**, or city hall, both designed by the Austrian architect Wilhelm Holzbauer and the Dutchman Cees Dam. In the passage between the *stadhuis* and the opera house, you'll find a replica of the Normaal

DISTRICTS

South Canals

0 ———— 400 m
0 ———— 400 yds

Stopera

©NBTC

Amsterdams Peil (standard watermark). The black marble **monument** standing in front of city hall, at the corner of the Amstel and the Zwanenburgwal, commemorates the resistance by Jewish citizens who lost their lives during World War II.

Jewish Quarter

East of the Waterlooplein lies the Jodenbuurt, the city's former Jewish quarter. Artist Rembrandt's house, now the **Museum Het Rembrandthuis★** *(see Old Masters)*, is situated in the heart of the old Jewish quarter. **Rembrandt** purchased his home in 1639.

Joods Historisch Museum★
Nieuwe Amstelstraat 1. Open daily 11am–5pm. Closed Rosh Hashanah and Yom Kippur. €9, children 13-17 €4.50, under 13 free. 020 531 0310. www.jhm.nl.

The Museum of Jewish History is housed in a complex of four synagogues on Jonas Daniël Meijerplein. The first one on the site was the Grote Synagogue, built in 1671, but as the congregation expanded, new ones were built on neighboring plots: the upstairs, or Obbene Sjoel, in 1685, the third, or Dritt Sjoel, in 1700 and the new or Nieuwe Synagogue in 1752. The latter is recognizable by the Ionic columns at the entrance and by the domed roof.

The **Nieuwe Synagoge** examines five aspects of the "Jewish identity": religion; Israel and Zionism; war, persecution and survival; history; and mixing of cultures. The **Grote Synagoge★** or Grand Synagogue still has the marble Ark of the Covenant given to the community in 1671. Various

Joods Historisch Museum

©Liselore Kamping/Joods Historisch Museum

themes, such as the Jewish Year and its feast days and the Bar Mitzvah, are explained through displays of items used in worship and ceremonials (silver plate, lamps, clothes, decorations for the Torah). The galleries are devoted to the socio-economic history of the Jewish people in the Netherlands. The renovation work brought to light a **mikveh★**, a bath used for ritual purification.

Portugese Synagoge★
Mr. Visserplein 3. Open Apr–Oct Sun–Fri 10am–4pm; Nov–Mar Sun–Thu 10am–4pm, Fri 10am–2pm. Closed on Jewish holidays. €6.50 children 13-17 €4, under 13 free. 020 624 5351. www.portugese synagoge.nl.

This massive brick building, lit by tall windows, was built in 1675 by Elias Bouman as a place of worship for three Portuguese congregations that had just united. The interior remains as shown in Emmanuel de Witte's painting

Portuguese Synagogue

in the Rijksmuseum, with wide wooden barrel vaults supported by high columns, galleries for the women, the Ark of the Covenant, and large **copper chandeliers**. There is no curtain *(parochet)* in this synagogue, as this feature was unknown in the Jewish tradition of Spain and Portugal.

Sand is regularly sprinkled on the floor to absorb the humidity and muffle the noise of footsteps and, just as in the 17C, the synagogue has no electricity or heating. Library Ets Haim–Livraria Montezinos, the oldest Jewish library in the world—and one of the most important—is attached to this place of worship.

De Dokwerker, the statue of a docker by **Mari Andriessen** on the square in front of the synagogue, commemorates the strike launched by the dockers on 25 February 1941 in protest against the deportation of Amsterdam's Jewish population.

Pintohuis

St. Antoniesbreestraat 69.

This 17C patrician mansion appears better suited to a spot on one of Amsterdam's resplendent canals. Indeed it was one of the first such residences to be erected on a landlocked street, the Sint Antoniesbreestraat, instead of on a canal.

While the mansion itself was built in the early years of the 17C, its illustrious façade, an example of **Holland Classicism**, dates from 1680s, when its namesake inhabitants moved in: the Portuguese-Jewish Pinto family, a well-to-do family of merchants and bankers that hobnobbed with statesmen and other city elite. The Pintohuis remained in the family's possession until the end of the 19C, but since then it has faced an uncertain future.

Currently it houses a branch of the Amsterdam Public Library *(open Mon, Wed, Fri, Sat see website for hours, which vary; 020 624 3184; www.oba.nl)*. Be sure to stop in to see the interior of the house, especially its exquisite ceiling decoration.

THE CANALS★★★

Today the city of Amsterdam has 165 canals. The most famous are the 25m/82ft wide Singel, Herengracht, Keizersgracht and **Prinsengracht**. Completed in the 16C and 17C, they stretch from the Brouwersgracht to the Leidsegracht. Most of the houses lining the canals in the center of the city were built by wealthy merchants in the 17C and 18C. Although somewhat similar in appearance, with their narrow façades and front steps, they differ in color and their gable decoration. Beams with pulleys project over the pediments: the narrow staircases make it impossible to bring in furniture. Here are descriptions of some houses and other attractions along these major canals. *Note: houses are numbered from the north end south to the Amstel River.*

Singel★★

This former moat became a canal in 1586. Tour highlights include the high-domed **Nieuwe Ronde Lutherse Kerk**, New Church or Round Lutheran Church (1671), now a concert hall and conference center; the house at **no. 7**, often said to be the narrowest in the city, but in fact, is the rear access to a house in Jeroenensteeg; and **Bloemenmarkt★★**, the flower market sitting at the Singel's end.

Herengracht★★★

This canal (1586–1609) is the most important of the four canals; the patricians who ruled 16C and 17C Amsterdam planted their opulent mansions here along the water. It was named for the Heren XVII, the 17 governors of the Dutch East India Company. Wealthy merchants also came here to live; their houses vie with one another in their rich decoration and gables.

Huis Bartolotti★

The Bartolotti House at Herengracht 170 was built by Hendrick de Keyser around 1617. The combination of brick and freestone on the front is typical of the Dutch Renaissance style.

Cromhouthuizen★

Philip Vingboons built this row of four houses (nos. 364, 366, 368

Houseboats and Amstel Hotel on the Herengracht

© Martin Moxter/age fotostock

and 370) with neck gables in 1662. The gracious buildings, Baroque in terms of their decoration, were commissioned by Catholic merchant Jacob Cromhout. Housed in a 17C canal house at no. 366 is the **Bijbels Museum** *(see Museums)*, or Bible Museum.

Nos. 386 to 394★

These houses present a lovely series of façades. At no. 394, below a graceful gable, a **façade stone** depicts the four sons of Aymon, mounted on their horse Bayard.

Gouden Bocht

The large, elegant houses on the second bend in the Herengracht are known collectively as the "Golden Bend." In the 17C, this area was prized by wealthy Amsterdam citizens who could afford double-fronted houses, now mostly occupied by banks and consulates.

Kattenkabinet

Open Mon–Fri 10am–4pm, Sat–Sun and holidays 11am–5pm. Closed 1 Jan, 30 Apr, 25–26 and 31 Dec. €6, children 4-12 €3. 020 626 9040. www.kattenkabinet.nl.
If you're a cat lover, don't miss the Cat Gallery, located in a 17C house at **no. 497**, where exhibits focus on works of art that show all manner of cats.

No. 476★

This elegant mansion was built around 1740. Its fine façade shows off six Corinthian pillars and decorative festoons. The open-work attic above the main part of the building has a balustrade adorned with the owner's blazon and an eagle above it.
The **ABN-AMRO Bank** building (1923), on the corner of Vijzelstraat, was designed by the architect **De Bazel**, a contemporary of Berlage.

Museum Willet-Holthuysen★

Open Mon–Fri 10am–5pm, Sat–Sun and holidays 11am–5pm. Closed 1 Jan, 30 Apr and 25 Dec. €8, children 6-18 €4, under 6 free. 020 523 1822. www.willetholthuysen.nl.
Completed in 1690, the mansion at no. 605 has a series of elegantly furnished rooms that provide a glimpse into the lifestyle of rich merchants of the time. The kitchens, the men's smoking room, the bedroom and the collector's room contain paintings, pottery, glassware and gold and silver. The **garden★** has been restored to the original design of Daniël Marot.

Keizersgracht★★

Hightlights of the 1612 Keizersgracht Canal are the restored 1622 brick house at no. 123, the **Huis met de Hoofden★**

🚢 Boat Tours

A boat tour offers an excellent view of the most important canals as well as part of the port. The route varies according to which locks are open. *For a tour, contact any of the following operators:* **Rederij Lovers**, *Prins Hendrikkade 25, 020 530 1090, www.lovers.nl;* **Rederij Kooij**, *opposite Rokin 125, 020 623 3810, www.rederijkooij.nl;* **Gray Line Amsterdam**, *Damrak Steiger 5 020 535 3308, www.graylineamsterdam.com;* **Amsterdam Canal Cruises**, *Nicolaas Witsenkade 1A, 020 626 5636, www.amsterdamcanalcruises.nl.*

whose façade is decorated with six sculpted heads of Roman gods (hence its name, "house of the heads"), and no. 672, the stately mansion housing the **Museum Van Loon**★ *(open Wed–Mon, 11am–5pm; €8, children 6-18 €4, under 6 free; 020 624 5255; www. museumvanloon.nl).* Built in 1671 by Adriaan Dortsman, the house once belonged to the painter **Ferdinand Bol** (1616–80). It has a stairwell decorated in stucco with magnificent **banisters**★ from the second half of the 18C, and numerous portraits. A small Classical-style coach house sits in the French-style **garden**★.

Prinsengracht★★

Highlights along this canal (1612) include the **Western Church** or the **Westerkerk**★ *(open Mon–Sat 11am–3pm; 020 624 7766; www.westerkerk.nl)* and the **Anne Frank Huis**★★ *(see Eternal Amsterdam).* Built between 1620 and 1631, the Renaissance-style church was designed by **Pieter de Keyser,** based on the plans of his father Hendrick. It is the largest

Huis met de Hoofden

©ATCB

Iconic Amsterdam Bridges

Amsterdam has constructed some 1,200 bridges to cross its rivers and canals. The **Magere Brug★** (Skinny Bridge), familiar to James Bond fans from the film *Diamonds Are Forever* (1971), is a drawbridge that links opposite banks of the Amstel River at Kerkstraat; its name refers to the original 13-arch bridge built here in 1691. The current Magere Brug dates from 1934, and looks most splendid after dark, when its white wooden body is illuminated by hundreds of tiny light bulbs. One bridge with two superlatives, the **Torensluis** is both the oldest (built in 1648) and widest, at 42m/138ft across; its generous width once supported a clock tower and prison, but is now bare save for a statue of 19C Dutch satirist Multatuli. Two recent bridges have been awarded the prestigious National Steel Prize (*Nationale Staalprijs*): the **Enneüs Heermabrug** (completed in 2000), whose steel curves undulate over the IJ River, and the **Nesciobrug** between Amsterdam and the town of Diemen (completed in 2006), whose sleek form has earned it the nickname "the eel." The so-called **Bridge of 15 Bridges** is a popular spot from which to admire the symmetry of these structures; from this bridge, located on Reguliersgracht and the corner of Herengracht, 14 others can be seen, thus, 15 in total.

Protestant church in the city. The remarkable carillon (*played Tue noon–1pm*) in the 85m/280ft **bell tower★★** dates from 1638 and is the work of **François Hemony**. Don't miss the **view★** from the top of the tower that takes in the central canals and the Jordaan district.

The church **interior** is quite plain; the nave has wooden barrel vaulting and the 12 chandeliers are copies of the originals.

The magnificent painted organ panels are the work of **Gerard de Lairesse**.

Rembrandt was buried here in 1669, one year after his son Titus, though the exact location of his tomb is not known.

On the pavement behind the church in **Westermarkt** square stands the **Homomonument**, commemorating gay men and women who died in the Nazi concentration camps.

Reguliersgracht★

Running perpendicular to the other four canals, and paralleling the Amstel River, this delightful canal, built in 1664, was named after the former convent of regular nuns. The idea of enclosing the canal in order to build a tram line was dropped, and the canal was given conservation protection. It provides one of the most attractive **views★★** of any of Amsterdam's waterways.

From the bridge spanning the canal beside Kerkstraat, you can see seven bridges—count them—across the Reguliersgracht.

THE PORT AREA

While the center may be the heart of the city, the port has historically been Amsterdam's lifeblood. It is bisected by Centraal Station into eastern and western halves, the small bodies of Oosterdok and Westerdok on either side. To the east, Science Center Nemo casts a shadow above the entrance to the IJ Tunnel, which pulses with traffic to Amsterdam North. Oostelijke Handelskade is dense with desirable destinations: renowned music venues, a mammoth library, a modern cruise-ship terminal, former warehouses converted to restaurants and cultural centers. To the west, the docklands stretch to the locks that lead to the North Sea. The Westerpark district houses a beloved summer market and a former factory recycled into an arts center. Nearby Museum het Schip celebrates the architecture of the Amsterdam School. Farther west, the Westerport district is now the center of harbor activity, thanks to its accessibility from the North Sea.

Eastern Docklands

See Map inside back cover.

Today these docklands are full of inventive architecture, an enviable assortment of boutiques and restaurants, and more than a few tourist-worthy attractions. It was not always so.

The **Oostelijke Havensgebied**, or Eastern Docklands, was dealt a bad hand by history: after World War II, the port was moved to the more spacious west to accommodate container ships and other super-sized new vessels. Deprived of its source of income, the Eastern Docklands became a no-man's-land until the 1980s, when the city began its development as a residential area.

Sometimes called "New East," these linked islands boast a state-of-the-art public library on the west. To the east, the **Piet Heinkade** crosses to the **Oostelijke Handelskade**, a narrow strip with dramatic architecture joined to KNSM Island in the north and the other Eastern Islands to the south and west. South of the Oostelijke Handelskade is a district laced with waterways and collectively known as the **Oostelijke Eilanden** (Eastern Islands) and **Kadijken**; here, **ARCAM** revisits Amsterdam's architectural evolution, while the National Maritime Museum, **Het Scheepvaartmuseum**, illustrates the country's use of water power to secure its prosperity. "Docked" above the IJ Tunnel is the hull-shaped Science Center **NEMO**, whose vast roof opens in summer for a panorama of Oosterdok.

©NBTC
Eastern Docklands

Openbare Bibliotheek Amsterdam, Youth Section

Openbare Bibliotheek Amsterdam★

Oosterdokskade 143. Open daily 10am–10pm. 020 523 0900. www.oba.nl.

This central branch of the Amsterdam Public Library has been widely applauded for its beauty, functionality and sustainability, all under one solar panel-clad roof. Architectural firm Jo Coenen & Co. designed the sleek, airy construction that opened in 2007 with all the amenities of a first-rate public library, and then some.

One Amazing Library

What are visitors treated to at the Openbar Bibliotheek? Open stacks, 600 computers and free Wi-Fi, for starters. Its 9.5 floors are divided by subject: Floor 5 houses an exhibit space, ticket vendor and cafe; Floor 1 caters to children. Several rooms are dedicated to luminaries of Dutch literature. Floor 7, the top floor, houses one of the library's more extraordinary features: an in-house cafeteria. Take your self-serve meal out on the terrace for one terrific view of the IJ River.

At 28,000sq m/301,389sq ft, the spacious complex receives nearly two million visitors per year. Overlooking the IJ River, the **Jo Coenen Terrace** was named for the building's chief architect.

Oostelijke Handelskade

This "Eastern Trade Quay" is a true example of Oosterdok's revival. Two parallel main streets, Veemkade and Piet Heinkade, traverse it west to east, each on the opposite shore of the narrow, artificial island. On the western point, the **Muziekgebouw aan het IJ** *(see Performing Arts)* offers classical music within a strikingly designed space. At the side, **Het Bimhuis** *(see Performing Arts)* is a world-class venue for jazz and improvisational music.

Just to the east rises **Passenger Terminal Amsterdam** *(Piet Heinkade 27; 020 509 1000; www.ptamsterdam.com)*, where some 200,000 visitors disembark each year. East of the terminal sit converted warehouses *(pakhuizen)* such as **Pakhuis de Zwijger** *(Piet Heinkade 179; 020 788 4433; www.dezwijger.nl)*, a self-proclaimed "warehouse for media

Passenger Terminal with Pazazz

The busy international cruise terminal, rising east of the Muziekgebouw, harbors a tourist information desk, shops and an eatery or two, a TV-viewing area, public telephones, Internet consoles (free access), ATM machines and luggage lockers. There's even a children's area. It is served by tram lines 25 and 26. Bikes *(see Practical Information)* and even Segways can be rented nearby.

and culture" that combines a restaurant-cafe with an arts center. Nearby Pakhuis Amsterdam houses British celebrity chef Jamie Oliver's restaurant **Fifteen** *(see Restaurants)*. Toward the far eastern side of the Oostelijke Handelskade, music venue **Panama** *(Oostelijke Handelskade 4; 020 311 8686; www.panama.nl)* attracts such international acts as Alicia Keys, Colbie Caillat and Timbaland. The monumental **Lloyd Hotel** *(Oostelijke Handelskade 34; see Hotels)* was built in 1918 to entice travelers to sail to South America on the Royal Holland Lloyd ship line, but the plan failed; after the company's bankruptcy, the Lloyd served various purposes until it was ultimately re-opened as a hotel in 2004. Another leftover from Royal Holland Lloyd, the company's former coffeehouse has been reincarnated as the restaurant **KHL** *(Oostelijke Handelskade 44; 020 779 1575; www.khl.nl)*, with a homey outdoor patio and live music.

Prins Hendrikkade

Modern-day Prince Hendrik Quay traces the IJ waterfront from central station to the area known as the Kadijken, and overlaps the northern perimeter of the former city wall. Several relics of that period still stand side-by-side with later architecture. Just southeast of Centraal Station, A.C. Bleijs's 19C

Sint Nicolaaskerk *(St. Nicholas Church, Prins Hendrikkade 73; Tue–Fri 11am–4pm, Mon & Sat noon–3pm; by donation; 020 624 8749; www.nicolaas-parochie.nl)* is a pastiche of neo-Baroque and neo-Renaissance features; visitors often stare up in wonderment at its 58m/190ft dome, which overshadows the narrow sidewalk below.

East of the Geldersekade rises the storied **Schreierstoren** *(Prins Hendrikkade 94-95)*, a stout 15C tower that stood where the city wall rounded a sharp corner, or *schreiershoek*, which had lent the tower its name. The fact that "schreierstoren" can also be understood as "weeper's tower" spawned the myth that this was the place where sailors' wives would bid their husbands farewell. Nowadays, the Schreierstoren is a restaurant and reception hall *(020 428 8291; www.schreierstoren.nl)* that can be rented for events; its nautical-themed VOC Café is open to the public.

On the corner of this quay and the Binnenkant stands the impressive **Scheepvaarthuis★**, or Shipping House. It was built in 1916 by the principal architects of the Amsterdam School, Van der Mey, Michel de Klerk and P.L. Kramer, and is considered the first product of this seminal architectural movement. Conceived as an office block, in 2007 it reopened its

©Wim Ruigrok/ARCAM

doors as the **Grand Hotel Amrâth** (*Prins Hendrikkade 108, see hotels*). Farther east, the Kalkmarkt runs southward, where it becomes **Oudeschans★**; here, one can see another trace of the medieval city wall, namely the early 16C **Montelbaanstoren** (*Oudeschans 2*). This defensive tower should be familiar to Rembrandt lovers, as it was a favorite subject of the painter; it was nicknamed Malle Jaap (Silly James) because of its clock tower, whose bells would ring out at odd hours of the day.

ARCAM
Prins Hendrikkade 600. Open Tue– Fri 1pm–5pm. 020 620 4878. www.arcam.nl.
Opposite the Scheepvaarthuis, on the other side of the IJ River, the **Architecture Center Amsterdam** lives up to its name as an authority on local architecture. Part library, part exhibition space (*see Architecture*), the center welcomes visitors to its uniquely contoured headquarters (built by René van Zuuk) to learn about Amsterdam architecture on-site, or to pick up one of the handy publications for use on a self-paced architectural tour. The ARCAM Panorama presents an illustrated history of Amsterdam's urban development from the year 800 to the present.

Eastern Islands and Kadijken
Oostelijke Eilanden and Kadijken are a series of adjacent islands just inland from the Eastern Docklands. Their occupants include an eclectic variety of lesser-known attractions plus a new star, the recently unveiled **Het Scheepvaartmuseum** (National Maritime Museum). To the east stands a little-known ecclesiastical jewel, the **Oosterkerk** (*Eastern Church, Kleine Wittenburgerstraat 1; 020 627 2280; www.oosterkerk-amsterdam.nl*), whose sober 17C Protestant interior now hosts concerts, exhibits and lectures. Smaller theaters dot the islands, such as **Het Werktheater** (*Oostenburgergracht 75; 020 627 0297; www.werkteater.com*) and the **Theater Fabriek Amsterdam** (*Czaar Peterstraat 213; 020 522 5260; www.theater*

fabriekamsterdam.nl), whose productions are typically in Dutch but their musical performances are suitable for all audiences.

The Kadijken, the southernmost islands that run from west to east, house a number of worthwhile stops. Chief of these is the **Werfmuseum 't Kromhout** *(Hoogte Kadijk 147; 020 627 6777; www.machinekamer.nl)*, a combination wharf and museum that invites the public to watch restoration and repair work on historic and modern ships during its limited hours *(Tue 10 am–5pm)*. On the southern perimeter, **Entrepotdok** is a complex of 84 warehouses built between 1708 and 1829 and rebuilt in the 1980s for mixed use. At the northeast point towers the **De Gooyer**, the Netherlands' tallest wooden windmill *(not open to the public)*.

Het Scheepvaartmuseum★★
Kattenburgerplein 1.

After a protracted renovation, the National Maritime Museum reopened to the public in fall 2011

Touring Tip

The De Gooyer may be permanently closed to the public, but the attached former bathhouse now holds the **IJ Brewery** *(Brouwerij 't IJ, Funenkade 7; 020 622 8325; www.brouwerijhetij.nl)* and pub. After musing over the mill from the outside, enter the pub to sample 🍺 **beer** brewed on the spot, nibble on smoked meats and cheeses, and take a free tour of the premises *(Fri and Sun 4pm)*.

in its water-borne home, a former warehouse of the Amsterdam Admiralty repurposed in 1973 as a museum. By the mid-17C, the Dutch Republic claimed the status of world naval power, and boasted more water and more ships than any other country. Fine art reflected the national pride in the Netherlands' naval prowess.

One museum exhibit tells the story of the port. *For a description of the collection, see For Kids.*

©Martin Waalboer/Het Scheepvaartmuseum

Het Scheepvaartmuseum, the National Maritime Museum

DISTRICTS

NEMO★

Oosterdok 2.

Bright green and shaped like the bow of a ship, this science center *(see Architecture)* was designed by Italian architect **Renzo Piano**. It provides hands-on displays on subjects as varied as medicine and money, and is particularly suitable for children *(see For Kids)*. There is a **view★★** of the city from the roof.

Haarlemmerbuurt and Western Islands

See Map inside back cover.

A narrow strip of land bordered to the north by railroad tracks and to the south by the Brouwersgracht canal, the Haarlemmerbuurt stretches westward from Centraal Station. Its chief attraction is the eclectic **Haarlemmerstraat** (which turns into Haarlemmerdijk), with its many boutiques, cafes, restaurants and coffee shops. On the northwest corner, **Kaasland** *(Cheeseland: Haarlemmerstraat 2; 020 422 1715; www.kaasland.com)* is a typical Dutch cheese shop where Gouda and Edam can be found. From here on, the street is overtaken by storefronts that boast retro and contemporary fashion, eateries that follow the culinary spectrum from continental to Indian and Tibetan cuisine, and niche retailers whose products run from condiments to chess paraphernalia. On the south side, the restored 17C **West-Indisch Huis** *(West Indies House, Herenmarkt 99)* will stop architecture lovers in their tracks: within this former headquarters of the Dutch West India Company, it was resolved to raise a fort on Manhattan in 1625. Another memento of the Dutch colony of

New Amsterdam is the bronze statue of Peter Stuyvesant. North of the train tracks, the Haarlemmerbuurt disperses into the **Western Islands**, each with only a handful of streets. There are no major attractions here, but visitors will spot noteworthy architecture, exhibition spaces and other surprises.

Galerie van Gelder

(Planciusstraat 9 A; open Tue–Sat, 1pm–5:30pm, and first Sun each month; 020 627 7419; www.galerie vangelder.com) showcases adventurous new art from the Netherlands and abroad at its location on the canal Smallepadsgracht.

The **Realeneiland** is lined with attractively maintained ware-houses; on Zandhoek, opposite the Westerdok, a row of restored 17C houses sports a series of animal-themed façade stones. On the Bickersgracht, the quaint little **Dierenkapel** *(Bickersgracht 207; open Tue–Sun 9am–5pm; 020 420 6855; www.bickersgracht. info)*, a so-called "children's farm" *(kinderboerderij)*, invites the young to learn about typical barnyard animals.

Spaarndammerbuurt

At the far western end of the Haarlemmerdijk, the **Haarlemmerpoort** (Haarlem Gate) arches over Haarlemmerplein (Haarlem Square); these similar names hint at the direction west to the provincial capital of Haarlem. Architect Bastiaan de Greef was inspired by Classical architecture for mid-19C Haarlemmerpoort: note the Corinthian columns that line its archway.

Museum het Schip

©Museum het Schip

Museum het Schip★
Spaarndammerplantsoen 140.
Open Tue–Sun 11am–5pm.
Tours on the hour. 020 418 2885.
www.hetschip.nl.

Northwest of Haarlem Square stands "The Ship" Museum. Despite its name and proximity to the harbor, this isn't a nautical museum, but an architectural one. Michel de Klerk, an architect of the 20C Amsterdam School, conceived the complex as a "palace for workers" that comprised apartments and facilities such as a post office; it would become one of the most celebrated achievements of the Amsterdam School. The museum arose from a temporary exhibit into a permanent testament of Het Schip's value as an architectural monument; a **model apartment** in the museum's tower allows visitors a window into the lives of the former inhabitants, while the post office contains the only intact **interior** from De Klerk, whose architecture is far more famous for its canonical exteriors.

Westerpark
South of the Spaarndammerbuurt, **Westerpark** (see Parks and Gardens) fans outward toward the district that bears its name. A converted factory, **Westergasfabriek** (Haarlemmerweg 8-10; www.westergasfabriek.nl) is now the popular site of concerts, exhibits, and yearly events; permanent amenities include assorted shops, cafes, restaurants and bars.

The monthly **Sunday market** (dates vary; www.sundaymarket.nl) on the premises allows shoppers to browse local produce, art and fashion to the sound of live musicians.

THE JORDAAN★

Sitting south of the Haarlemmerbuurt and just outside the western canal belt, this peaceful but lively district shows off canal-laced streets filled with restaurants and cafes, boutiques and art studios behind its 17C façades. Few would associate the Jordaan of today with the abject poverty that characterized it as late as the 20C, when dilapidated tenements—now restored into monuments—were crowded with four times its current population. Penniless artists were a common fixture in the community, not least of all a bankrupt Rembrandt, who died here and was buried at the local Westerkerk (Western Church).

The attractions of the district are two historic churches (the Noorderkerk and Westerkerk), a number of small-scale museums, splendidly restored façades and *hofjes* (inner courtyards), and the overall atmosphere of its streets, canals and bruin cafes.

Grachts Galore

See Map inside back cover.

Brouwersgracht★

The Brewers' Canal, which marks the northern boundary of the Jordaan, is lined with attractively restored warehouses like **nos. 172 to 212**. De Kroon warehouse, **no. 118**, has a carved stone on its façade depicting a crown, which is what its name means. A row of houses with crow-stepped gables dating from 1641 stand near the bridge where Brouwersgracht and Prinsengracht meet. The popular **Papeneiland** cafe is located here.

Egelantiersgracht★

This canal, with its beautiful 17C and 18C houses, has retained the typical charm of yesteryear. Like the Bloemgracht, it has become a sought-after address.

Bloemgracht★

This canal, sometimes ironically called the Herengracht of the Jordaan, used to be occupied by dyers and paint makers. Three magnificent houses, nos. 87 to 91, have stepped gables. Many others have **façade stones**: look for a pelican (no. 19), unicorn (no. 23), trout (no. 34) and sower (no. 77).

Hidden Hofjes

The Jordaan proliferates with *hofjes* (pronounced "HOF-yes"), communal inner **courtyards** around which residences were built for seniors, laborers, the poor or others. Those still existing are typically listed monuments that have been preserved, and are often inhabited by private individuals.

Not all *hofjes* are accessible to the public; one spectacular example that is open for discreet visitors to take a look around is the **Sint Andrieshof** *(Egelantiersgracht 105-141)*, built in 1616 as an almshouse for elderly Roman Catholics. Similarly, the **Nieuwe Suykerhofje** *(Prinsengracht 383-393)*, also open, was established in 1755 as a sanctuary for Roman Catholic females. Filled with almshouses, the **Karthuizerhofje** *(Karthuizersstraat 89-171)* is the largest in Amsterdam, built in 1650 by the municipal architect Daniël Stalpart. The **Claes Claeszoon Hofje** *(Eerste Egelantiersdwarsstraat 1-5)* is a 17C almshouse with a picturesque inner courtyard.

MUST SEE

Interior, Houseboat Museum

©ATCB

Markets, Museums and More
See Map inside back cover.

Noordermarkt Square
The 1623 Protestant **Noorderkerk** *(open Sat–Mon; www.noorderkerk. org)* was completed by **Hendrick de Keyser** and his son, Pieter, to serve the northern Jordaan; its shape is a Greek cross, each of whose four equal arms ends in a church tower. Here on the **Noordermarkt** square, members of the Dutch resistance coordinated the February Strike in protest to the Nazi's anti-Jewish measures; a plaque on the south face of the church honors the strike; another commemorates the "Jordaanese" who perished in the war. Noordermarkt is the site of a weekly farmer's market.

Museums of the Jordaan
One of the most popular destinations in Amsterdam, the **Anne Frank Huis** *(see Eternal Amsterdam)*, lies on the perimeter of the Jordaan *(Prinsengracht 263-267)*. The narrow-fronted house, built in 1635, includes the "secret annexe," where Anne and her family hid out from the Nazis. The **Houseboat Museum** *(Prinsengracht 296K; open daily 11am–5pm; closed Jan 1 and 9-12, Apr 30 and Dec 25, 26 and 31; €3.50, children up to 152cm €2.75; www.houseboatmuseum.nl)* is, as the name implies, dedicated to the familiar Dutch phenomenon of the houseboat. Visitors are invited aboard the *Hendrika-Maria* to learn the ins and outs of life on an Amsterdam houseboat. Another curiously-themed Jordaan museum is the **Pianola Museum** *(Westerstraat 106; Sun 2pm–5pm; €5, children €3; www.pianola.nl)*, a tribute to the automatic piano that rose to popularity in the early 20C; the permanent collection contains a variety of pianolas and 25,000 rolls of the perforated sheet music the instruments read. Occasional concert series allow audiences to hear these now rare instruments in live performance.

THE PLANTAGE★

Situated to the east of city center, this residential area was developed in the late 19C. For many years it was home to the wealthiest members of the Jewish community. Of French origin, Plantage takes its name from the area's many parks and gardens. *See Map inside back cover.*

Hortus Botanicus★
Plantage Middenlaan 2A.
See Parks And Gardens. Created in 1682 for the cultivation of medicinal plants, the botanical garden also has a greenhouse representing three different climatic zones, and a palm house.

De Burcht
Henri Polaklaan 9. 020 624 1166. www.deburcht.nl.
The former headquarters of the Dutch diamond workers' union, founded in 1894 by Henri Polak, was for years the home of the Nationaal Vakbondsmuseum (National Trade Union Museum). Since the museum's collection was absorbed by another institution, De Burcht is only occasionally open

to the public for lectures and other events; but it remains an important architectural landmark.
The imposing building was designed in 1900 by **Hendrik Petrus Berlage**, and soon gained the nickname of Burcht van Berlage (Berlage's Castle), a play on the name of the architect's iconic **Beurs van Berlage** *(see Performing Arts)* on the Damrak. The magnificent **staircase★** with its Art Deco **chandelier★**, the council chamber and the boardroom are all worth seeing.

Artis★★
Plantage Kerklaan 38-40.
Founded in 1838, Artis is one of Europe's oldest zoos *(see For Kids).*

Verzetsmuseum

©Verzetsmuseum

Muiderpoort

©ATCB

Verzetsmuseum★
Plantage Kerklaan 61. Open Tue–Fri 10am–5pm, Sat–Sun and public holidays 11am–5pm. Closed 1 Jan, 30 Apr and 25 Dec. €7.50, children 7-15 €4, under 7 free. 020 620 2535. www.verzetsmuseum.org.

This interactive museum uses sound recordings, photographs, film and a wide range of authentic objects to lead visitors on a journey through the occupied Netherlands of World War II. The horrors of people's daily lives during that wartime period are vividly brought to light.

As visitors walk along the reconstructed streets, they are given answers to questions such as what happened on the ground in an air raid?; how did the propaganda machine of Nazi Germany operate?; and how did the resistance movement manage to get secret messages through? Letters of farewell thrown from deportation trains and yellow Stars of David recall the deportation of more than 100,000 Jews. The resourcefulness of people during times of war is illustrated through items such as radios, chess sets and small Christmas trees, all made by prisoners of war while in confinement.

Hollandsche Schouwburg
Plantage Middenlaan 24. Open daily 11am–4pm. Closed Rosh Hashanah and Yom Kippur. 020 531 0380. www.hollandsche schouwburg.nl.

This former theater was used during the war as a transit camp for Jews, and has a memorial to those who died.

Muiderpoort
Sarphatistraat 500.

The Muiderpoort (Muider Gate, built 1770) served as an entrance to the city in the 17C and 18C; its classical appearance is meant to evoke a triumphal arch, embellished with Doric elements. Napoleon entered the city in 1811 via the Muiderpoort.

DE PIJP

This area is actually an island linked to the rest of the city by 16 bridges. Nestled between Amsterdam Center and Amsterdam Oost (East), it is neatly bounded by the Stadshouderskade to the north, the Amstelkade to the south, the Amstel River to the east and the Ruysdaelkade to the west. A working-class area in the 19C, "the pipe," so nicknamed for its long, narrow streets (filled-in canals, in fact), now embraces a cosmopolitan population responsible for its current status as the "Latin Quarter" of Amsterdam. While often associated with two major tourist attractions, the Heineken Experience and Albert Cuypmarkt (Albert Cuyp Market), the Pijp is a lively area full of cafes, restaurants and shops concentrated especially around Frans Halsstraat, Ferdinand Bolstraat and Gerard Doustraat—three streets that take their name from celebrated 17C Dutch artists.

Heineken Experience

Stadhouderskade 78. Visit by 1hr self-guided tour daily 11am–7pm. Last ticket sales 5:30pm. Closed 1 Jan, 30 Apr and 25–26 Dec. €16, children 1-15 €1 per year of age (maximum €12). 020 523 9222. www.heinekenexperience.com.
In 1864 Gerard Adriaan Heineken founded the famous brewery. It closed in 1988 when operations moved to larger plants. The tour describes company history and brewing methods. Visitors see large copper stills and the stables and sample beer at tour's end.

Albert Cuypmarkt★

Albert Cuypstraat.
Open Mon–Sat, 9am–5pm.
www.albertcuypmarkt.com.
This large, colorful market *(see Shopping)* on the 3km/1.8mi long Albert Cuypstraat has been in existence since 1904; it sells just about anything from fruit to clothing from all over the world.

De Dageraad

©ATCB

A Multicultural "Latin Quarter"

De Pijp is Amsterdam at its most multicultural; some 150 ethnicities co-exist on this island, as the diverse wares of its popular Albert Cuyp Market attest. Guest workers from Morocco, Turkey, Suriname and elsewhere started to arrive here in the mid-20C, and since then have imbued the area with influences from their respective home countries. De Pijp's affordability has made it an attractive option to students and cash-conscious bons vivants, hence its reputation as the "Latin Quarter" of Amsterdam. See all these walks of life intersect at peaceful Sarphatipark (see Parks and Gardens) in the center of De Pijp.

Hotel Okura
Ferdinand Bolstraat 333.
020 678 7111. www.okura.nl.
One of the Netherlands' top business hotels (see Hotels), the Okura isn't just for business travelers; it has earned a name for itself as a culinary hot spot in Amsterdam. From the top of its 23 stories, one of the city's most spectacular **views** can be enjoyed.

Badcuyp Centrum voor Muziek
Eerste Sweelinckstraat 10. Show-times vary; lunch Sat–Sun from 1pm, dinner Tue–Sun 5:30–9:30pm.
020 675 9669. www.badcuyp.nl.
Jazz and world music lovers should not miss the opportunity to enjoy dinner and a 🎵 **show** at this venue that introduces a variety of new talent to audiences. Doubling as a cafe and restaurant, the center prides itself on sustainable, but affordable, lunch and dinner dishes that strive to be as international as its musical acts. On Wednesdays and Thursdays, diners are treated to live music and special deals.

De Appel
Eerste Jacob van Campenstraat 59 (entrance around the corner on Ferdinand Bolstraat). Open Tue–Sun 11am–6pm. Closed 30 Apr, 25 Dec and between exhibits.
€7, children 12-18 €3.50, under 12 free. www.deappel.nl.
The Appel arts center is a pioneer in the Dutch contemporary art scene: founded in 1975, it provided some of the first institutional support for new media such as installation and video art, and continues to foster new artists who represent a variety of disciplines, media and countries. De Appel hosts six exhibitions per year, which it supplements with (often free) tours, lectures and other educational activities.

De Dageraad★
Area around Pieter Lodewijk Takstraat.
North of the Amstel Canal, this complex of 350 workers' apartments was built between 1919 and 1922 by **Michel de Klerk** and **Piet L. Kramer** for the De Dageraad housing association. A stroll within the complex enables visitors to appreciate one of the most amazing working-class housing estates of the inter-war years. The unusual forms, undulating orange-tile roofs and rounded beige brick façades make it one of the finest products of the **Amsterdam School** of architecture.

AMSTERDAM OOST

Amsterdam East clearly revels in its own multiculturalism, both in its institutions and on its streets. The exquisite Tropenmuseum is a treasure trove of cultural artifacts from equatorial lands. Just a few blocks south, the diverse population shows its colors at the Dappermarkt, where rows of stalls peddle exotic foodstuffs and merchandise from Suriname, Turkey, North Africa and elsewhere—a real "world market," as it calls itself. On sunny days, visitors can take their market finds and picnic at the tranquil Oosterpark, which has two resplendent churches at its northern corners.

Oosterpark

See Map inside back cover.
Oosterpark is both the name of an urban park and the area that surrounds it. Unveiled in 1891, the 12ha/30acre **Oosterpark** was formerly the site of a cemetery that had to be relocated, amid much protest. Now a popular recreational spot, the park *(see Parks and Gardens)* has several monumental sculptures, most notably the **National Slavery Monument**, which commemorates the 1863 abolition of slavery in the former Dutch colonies. Two picturesque churches edge the park's perimeter: the Protestant **Muiderkerk** *(Linnaeusstraat 37; 020 668 2202; www.muiderkerk.nl)*, or rather its tower—the only structural element to survive a disastrous 1989 fire (it is cleverly embedded in a more modern complex on the Linnaeusstraat); the Reformed **Oosterparkkerk** *(Oosterpark 4, 020 665 0780; www.oosterparkkerk.nl)* bears the imprint of architect Abraham Salm, who built the monumental aquarium at Artis zoo *(see For Kids)*. The city has recently conceived a plan to expand the park northward; when completed, the new addition will encompass several protected monuments north of the current park.

Tropenmuseum★
Linnaeusstraat 2. Open daily 10am–5pm (til 3pm 5, 24 & 31 Dec. Closed 1 Jan, 30 Apr, 5 May and 25 Dec. €9, children 6-18 €5, under 6 free. 020 568 8200. www. tropenmuseum.nl.
Part of the Royal Tropical Institute, the museum is an excellent source of information about the cultures of Africa, Asia, Oceania, Latin America and the Middle East. Displays include everyday objects, works of art, reconstructions of homes and shops, photographs, slide shows, all working together to give visitors an insight into life in tropical and subtropical countries. The **children's museum** holds two-year exhibits for youngsters.

Dappermarkt
Dapperstraat.
Mon–Sat 9am–6pm.
One of the city's liveliest markets and certainly its most multicultural, the Dappermarkt comprises more than 250 stalls stretching along Dapperstraat. Firmly rooted in the local community, it serves the diverse ethnicities that live in the immediate vicinity, the Dapperbuurt, and elsewhere in Amsterdam East, with an assortment of international foodstuffs and other items.

AMSTERDAM NOORD

Without a doubt, the area on the banks of the IJ River north of Centraal Station is an underrated part of the city. It appeals to a variety of tastes. Art lovers throng its exhibition spaces, especially studios, which collectively welcome the public each year to the Open Atelierroute Boven het IJ; some are open all year. Foodies should stop at the Landmarkt (Schellingwouderdijk; www.landmarkt.nl), **a farmers' market filled with locally sourced meats and produce as well as** ambachtelijk **(artisanal) delicacies. Festival enthusiasts will want to find an excuse to visit the NDSM-werf** (Neveritaweg 61; www.ndsm.nl), **a former shipyard that is now the site of some of Amsterdam's most talked-about festivals and other live events.**

Noord's Novelties

Museum Amsterdam Noord
Zamenhofstraat 28A. Open Fri 1pm–5pm, Sat–Sun 11am–5pm. €3, children up to 16 €1.50. www.museumamsterdamnoord.nl.
This erstwhile public bathhouse is now an institution that documents the vibrant past and present of the vast district north of the IJ River. Themed exhibits dedicated to the arts, architecture, industry and other facets of Amsterdam Noord allow visitors to see the local attractions first-hand, with an emphasis on local artists. Tours are docent-led or self-guided (with one of the museum's informative brochures). The museum's Café du Nord offers a traditional local specialty, sweet white bread known as duivekater.

Wooden Houses
While it's popularly believed that only two wooden houses survive in Amsterdam (Begijnhof 34 and Zeedijk 1), this number fails to include the myriad monumental wooden houses that still stand north of the IJ River; indeed, these account for more than 100 of the district's rijksmonumenten (royal monuments).

They include not only houses but also wooden barns and even churches. Amsterdam's smallest church, the **Doopsgezinde Gemeente** (Menonite Parish, Meerpad 9; 020 636 9330; www.vdga.nl), is one such wooden monument, built by architect Piet Kater in 1843. Monumental dijkhuizen (dike houses) from the 17C to the 19C are concentrated on the Nieuwendammerdijk and Buiksloterdijk.

Touring Tip

Free ferries that depart from behind the Centraal Station (one to four times per hour) whisk visitors to various points north of the IJ River, from which expansive Amsterdam Noord can be explored on foot, or better still, by bike.
Bicycles can be taken on the ferry; the most convenient option is to rent one from the several bike rental facilities near Centraal Station (see Practical Information). Once you are in Noord, you can rent from Fietsreparatie Amsterdam, Meerpad 2, 061 399 8675, www.fietsreparatieamsterdam.nl.

ETERNAL AMSTERDAM

Amsterdam is a water-dominated city, threaded by both the IJ and Amstel rivers and the many canals that divide it into different quarters. The city is also famous for architecture, particularly the stepped façades of its tall brick houses, and the magnificent museums that contain works by some of the country's great masters. What attractions are iconic about this city, that define it for all time? We've chosen the following five sights as symbols of Amsterdam's uniqueness, as places and things that spring to mind when those who have been here want to remember its eternal essence.

THE CANALS★★★ AND HOUSEBOATS

One of the best ways of getting to know this unusual metropolis is to stroll along the picturesque **canals** with their narrow brick houses. The canals constitute the very soul of Amsterdam, flowing between age-old quaysides and drawing people from all over the world. For Amsterdam is a city built with water, the one element that represented a threat—and a blessing, for it provided the city with its great wealth. Another typical feature of the city is the numerous **houseboats** moored on the canals. They are one solution to the difficulty of building new housing in the old city center.

Birth of a City
Amstel's Castle

About 1205 Gijsbrecht van Amstel built a castle near the confluence of the **Amstel** and **IJ** rivers. To contain the Zuiderzee marshes to the north (now the IJsselmeer, a freshwater lake), the **first dike** (dam or *dijk* in Dutch) was constructed in 1222 between the south bank of the IJ and the Amstel.

The First Dikes

Two more dikes were built, and eventually "Amstelledamme" functioned as a lock, enabling the Amstel to flow into the IJ, when the IJ no longer presented the risk of flooding. In 1275 the town that had grown up on the banks was

Canal aglow at night

©NBTC

Houseboats crowd a canal

©ATCB

officially exempted from custom duties on goods carried along its waterways and **trade** flourished.

Population Increases

Once the economy had begun to develop, measures had to be taken to cope with the expanding population; the only solution was to reclaim the land by extending the embankments of the first dikes. By 1420, the townspeople still felt cramped, so they began to dig canals parallel to the river embankments. The entire 15C was devoted to this project.

Canal Expansion

By 1580 Amsterdam, overcrowded again, was the largest town in the Low Countries. In 1586 the town council decided to launch the building of the **Grachtengordel** (*gracht* means "canal" and *gordel* "belt"), a vast ring of four canals *(see Districts)* that is now a UNESCO World Heritage Site.

Originally created in 1425, the **Singel** canal was widened, and three new canals were built from 1586 to 1612. In 1662 the ring was extended eastward to the Amstel. By 1665 the work was finished, and the town once again doubled in size.

Continued Growth

Since the 1960s and 70s, the city has seen the development of such modern suburbs as **Buitenveldert** to the south and **Bijlmermeer** to the southeast. However, the housing problem remains acute, and the city is continuing to expand (Java-eiland, KNMS-eiland). **Amsterdam North**, beyond Centraal Station, is becoming the most populous district in the city.

Houseboat Homes

The 3,000 or so houseboats lining the 36km/22mi of Amsterdam's quays are one answer to the housing shortage.

Today city-owned boats patrol the canals to pick up any flotsam, and barges dredge the canal beds to keep the water clean.

But Amsterdam's canal waters are not safe for swimming; for years they have been used as a dumping ground for discarded items, and up until recently, open sewage from houseboats.

Unlawful Dumping

Since 2005, it has been illegal for houseboats to dump waste into surface water; by 2018 all of Amsterdam's houseboats are to be connected to sewer lines.

Experience the Canals

Take a boat ride

The colorful houseboats, tall medieval buildings and sheer size of the port are best seen from the water. The view of the **Reguliersgracht's** seven bridges alone makes the tour worth every minute. Not all tours offer the same route; ask about itineraries *(see Ideas and Tours, Boat Tours)*.

Tour a houseboat

The **Houseboat Museum** on the Prinsengracht *(no. 296K; open Mar–Oct Tues–Sun 11am–6pm, Nov–Feb Fri–Sun only; closed 1 Jan, 30 Apr and Dec 25, 26 & 31; €3.50, children €2.75; 020 427 0750; www. houseboatmuseum.nl)* is a former freighter transformed, in 2008, into a moored, spacious home.

Rent a houseboat

Converted barges have many amenities, including a kitchen, a shower, bedrooms, even a washer/dryer. Preview interiors and rates at www.houseboathotel.nl, www. houseboat-rental-amsterdam.com and other websites.

RIJKSMUSEUM★★★

Jan Luijkenstraat 1. Open daily 9am–6pm. Closed 1 Jan. €12.50, 18 and under free. 020 674 7000. www.rijksmuseum.nl.

See Map inside front cover. Meaning "state museum," the world-class Rijksmuseum was founded by Louis Bonaparte, Napoleon's brother, in 1808. In 1806 Napoleon made his brother King of Holland. Louis chose to live in Amsterdam, which became the capital of the kingdom.

Today the Rijksmuseum is known for its exceptional national collection of 15C to 17C Dutch paintings, including works by Rembrandt (*The Night Watch*), portraits by Frans Hals, the famous skies of Ruysdael and masterpieces by Vermeer. Other highlights of the collections are the assemblage of Chinese porcelain, Japanese ceramics, and art from India and Indonesia. These treasures are housed in an imposing, turreted building completed in 1885 and designed by **P. J. H. Cuypers** combining a Neo-Gothic and Neo-Renaissance style.

Rijksmuseum

©Arie de Leeuw/Rijksmuseum

MUST SEE

Exhibit, Anne Frank Huis

©Cris Toala Olivares/Anne Frank House

ANNE FRANK HUIS★★

Prinsengracht 263-267. Open mid-Mar–mid-Sept daily 9am–9pm (Sat and Jul–Aug til 10pm); rest of the year daily 9am–7pm (Sat til 9pm). Closed Yom Kippur. €9, children 10-17 €4.50, under 10 free. 020 556 7100. www.annefrank.org. Note: Long lines form in summer, so it's best to arrive early or purchase advance tickets online.

Today the Anne Frank Huis is one of the most visited attractions in Amsterdam.

Built in 1635, the narrow four-story merchant building at Prinsengracht 263 extends back a considerable way; behind it, there is an extension, or annex, that was enlarged in 1740. This building was not Anne Frank's home, but rather the place of her father's business *(see sidebar below)*.

It is estimated that 25,000 Dutch Jews went into hiding during the Nazi occupation of the Netherlands after the Dutch were defeated by the Germans in May 1940, during World War II. Anne was 13 years old when she and her family hid away. Slated for demolition, the building stood empty until the late 1950s when a foundation stepped in to preserve it. In 1960 the Anne Frank museum opened to the public. A revolving bookcase reveals a secret passage that leads to the bare rooms in the annex where the family hid. In the attic and in an adjoining house are exhibits on Anne's life, and on war, Nazism and anti-Semitism, as well as temporary displays related to these issues.

Anne and Her Family

A German Jew who emigrated from Frankfurt, Germany, to the Netherlands in 1933, **Otto Frank** began preparations to protect his family from growing Nazi persecution of Jews. He amassed a supply of food and hid himself, seven members of his family and friends (five adults and three children) in the annex in July 1942. But after two years of hiding, the Franks were betrayed, arrested and sent to a concentration camp in Auschwitz in August 1944; only the father returned. Anne and her sister died of typhoid fever just months before the liberation.

ETERNAL AMSTERDAM

How Did Holland Get into the Flower Business, Anyway?

The tulip is said to have been brought from Turkey by Augier Ghislain de Busbecq, the imperial envoy, in the late 16C. He gave bulbs to Charles de l'Ecluse, aka **Carolus Clusius**, a scientist in charge of the emperor's garden of medicinal plants in Vienna. Clusius began cultivating tulips on the sandy and humid soil that stretched along the North Sea between Leiden and Haarlem. Other flowers such as hyacinths and gladioli were introduced, but the tulip attained the highest prices. Between 1634 and 1636 speculation was rife, and "tulipmania" reached insane proportions. A rare tulip bulb sold for 6,000 florins (more than a million dollars today). Buyers would even exchange one bulb for a coach and two horses, or for a house. The Dutch States put an end to this speculation, and the flower industry was subsequently regulated.

The diary kept by Otto's daughter was found in the house; it displays a rare sensitivity. Her father published it in 1947. Since then, it has been translated into 65 languages and more than 30 million copies have been sold.

🌷 BLOEMENMARKT★★

On the Singel, between the Muntplein and Koningsplein. Open Mon–Sat 9am–5:30pm, Sun 11am–5:30pm.

Numerous flower stalls are dotted around Amsterdam, although the most picturesque are these **open-air stalls** on the Singel. The famous Bloemenmarkt, begun in 1862, is Amsterdam's floating flower market, the only one of its kind in the world; the stalls are set up on barges that are semi-permanently fixed to the canal walls. Its 15 stalls span an uninterrupted section of the Singel of about 220m/241 yards in length (about three city blocks). It caters primarily to tourists, who come here to see and purchase thousands of blooms of every color and type to take home. At these flower stalls and garden shops, all sorts of fresh cut flowers, seed packets, cuttings, potted plants and bulbs as well as garden tools and souvenirs are for sale. In addition to tulips in many colors,

Flower bulbs, Bloemenmarkt

there are daisies, gardenias, roses, lilies and hyacinths as well as exotic tropical plants from afar, to name just a few. In December the market also sells evergreen trees for the Christmas season.

THE WALLETJES★★

Amsterdam has some of the best nightlife in the world: cozy "brown cafes," trendy alternative bars, discos, nightclubs, and of course, the infamous **red-light district**, the Walletjes, known for prostitutes and drug-selling **coffee shops**. In this outward-looking country, **prostitution** (but not street prostitution) is legal, and so-called coffee shops selling soft drugs are tolerated. Prostitutes are not required to have health checks. The somewhat bell-shaped red-light district, awash with red neon signs, is bounded roughly by Centraal Station on the north, Damstraat to the south, Zeedijk on the east and Warmoesstraat on the west. Its long, narrow streets, draped with trees, are filled with 14C architecture that encompasses the Waag and two churches: Sint Nicolaaskerk and the Oude Kerk. The street called **Zeedijk** was known in the 15C for catering to sailors ashore from East India Company ships, in search of company and a drink. In the 16C the area was the residence of the city's wealthy merchants. Though a haven for prostitution for some 700 years, the once-seedy area is changing. Now a magnet for **organized crime**, the district has been targeted in the last several years by local authorities for clean-up, especially to counter human trafficking; the majority of prostitutes come from other

countries, including Eastern Europe and Africa.

There are theaters with live pornography, peep shows with video booths, an erotic museum, a marijuana museum, shops selling sex toys, and prostitutes legally soliciting from behind tall windows. Though the district will, no doubt, be preserved, it is well on the way to being scaled down. Many storefronts stand empty, soon to be occupied by fashion boutiques and art galleries if the city fathers have their way.

©Greg Gladman/Apa Publications

The Walletjes

ETERNAL AMSTERDAM

CAFES AND TEAROOMS

Amsterdam is believed to have more than a thousand cafes, known for their conviviality and cozy atmosphere. All of them, from grand designer cafes to traditional bruin cafes, provide a friendly place where most everyone chats with each other. Some serve snacks and simple meals, sometimes indicated by the word "eetcafé" in the window. Leidseplein and Rembrandtplein are particularly busy with cafe-goers. The area around the Stadsschouwburg (municipal theater) has a wealth of cafes. City center and the Jordaan boast the most authentic brown cafes, and tearooms can also be found in the city.

Bruin Cafes

Literally translated as "brown cafes," these dark-paneled bars are typical of the Netherlands. Characteristic of a cozy sitting room, they are famous for their welcoming atmosphere. Although some food is usually available, these cafes are more a place for drinking and relaxing rather than eating. The term derives from the smoky stains that accumulated on the walls, although nowadays such a color is more likely to have come from a tin of brown paint. Here are some brown cafes to sample.

Café Hoppe
Spui 18–20. 020 420 4420.
www.cafehoppe.com.
Hoppe is known as a meeting place for writers, journalists and other denizens of the literary world; in summer, customers spill out onto the pavement, creating "stand-up receptions."

Eijlders
Korte Leidsedwarsstraat 47.
020 624 2704. www.eijlders.nl.
With its regular afternoon poetry-readings, this well-loved cafe attracts literary types and locals. Despite its location next door to the bustling, touristy **Leidseplein★**, it's a haven of calm in comparison to its Irish bar counterparts, and the drinks are cheaper too. The artwork on the walls changes every few weeks.

't Gasthuys
Grimburgwal 7. 020 624 8230.
www.gasthuys.nl.
Sitting in the same location for more than 30 years, this brown cafe is especially popular with students from the nearby university. It serves both lunch and dinner as well as alcoholic drinks, and in summer offers patrons a terrace that overlooks the canal.

Café Hoppe

©Greg Gladman/Apa Publications

't Papeneiland
Prinsengracht 2, Jordaan. 020 624 1989. www.papeneiland.nl.
One of the city's most romantic brown cafes, this place has Delft tile decoration, an old-fashioned stove and a mezzanine level. The clientele are nearly as old as the walls here, but that aspect only adds to the atmosphere.

't Smalle
Egelantiersgracht 12, Jordaan. 020 623 9617. www.t-smalle.nl.
The clue is in the name of this tiny brown cafe overlooking the canal. It's a great spot for *gluhwein* (mulled wine) in winter, especially if the canals freeze and there's snow on the ground.

Grand Cafes
Reminiscent of the large, open cafes found on a Parisian boulevard, Amsterdam's grand cafes are the opposite of the intimate brown cafes. Spacious and light, they're the perfect place for coffee, and a croissant while reading the morning newspaper.

Café Americain
Leidsekade 97. 020 556 3000. www.edenamsterdamamerican hotel.com.
Part of the grand, historic American Hotel, the cafe is something of an Amsterdam institution. Despite its high prices, this brasserie is a must for lovers of Art Deco, with everything from the windows to the coffee cups exuding the period's inimitable style.

Café Amstelhoeck
Zwanenburgwal 15, Waterlooplein area. 020 620 9039. www.amstelhoeck.nl

This large cafe boasts a terrace right on the Amstel River, and a separate reading area. It's a good place to put your feet up after a visit to the Waterlooplein flea market just up the road.

Café Luxembourg
Spui 24. 020 620 6264. www.luxembourg.nl.
Part brown cafe and part French-style grand cafe, the Luxembourg serves everything from breakfast to beer in the evening. At its best late morning, the cafe is great for people-watching on Spui square.

Café de Jaren
Nieuwe Doelenstraat 20, Nieuwe Zijde. 020 625 5771. www.cafedejaren.nl.
This huge, modern, split-level cafe is particularly popular with young locals, especially students from the nearby university buildings. Its delightful two-level terrace on the Amstel River gets packed in fine weather.

Do Snack before Dinner

The city's cafes are especially inviting in the early evening when drinks are accompanied by tasty pre-dinner snacks called *borrelhapjes*. These snacks can be cold, such as small cubes of Dutch cheese and slices of raw or smoked beef sausage (*ossenworst*) and liver sausage (*leverworst*). Hot *borrelhapjes* are generally deep-fried and include mini spring rolls (*loempias*), cheese sticks rolled in filo pastry (*kaasstengels*), and the famous breaded filled meatballs (*bitterballen*). Dip them in mustard, but beware of burning your tongue.

Coffee Shops

You can go into a coffee shop just for a drink, but their main purpose is to sell hashish and marijuana, sold in bags by weight, or ready-rolled joints. For nonsmokers, most coffee shops sell "hash cakes," often in the form of chocolate brownies made with small quantities of hashish. Be careful: the drugs can be deceptively strong. Remember too that, while marijuana is tolerated in coffee shops, it is not legal to smoke it in the street, in other bars or cafes, or in public places in general. Nor is it widely accepted by the locals. Coffee shops in the Netherlands selling soft drugs are not technically legal but fall under a policy of tolerance (*gedoogbeleid*). Recently many coffee shops, being located too close to schools, have been shut down in Amsterdam.

Proeflokalen

Proeflokalen are a holdover from the 17C, when merchants came to sample drinks being sold by importers; *proeflokaal* means "tasting place." The local juniper-based spirit, called *jenever*, comes in various forms: young *jenever* resembles gin; the old (*corenwijn*) tastes like smooth whiskey. Ask to taste it before you buy.

De Admiraal

Herengracht 319. 020 625 4334.
www.proeflokaaldeadmiraal.nl.
The interior of de Admiral is slightly kitsch, with wooden barrels forming make-shift tables around the room. Its canal-side location makes it a popular venue, especially in summer. This *proeflokaal* makes its own *jenever* in one of Amsterdam's oldest distilleries.

De Drie Fleschjes

Gravenstraat 18. 020 624 8443.
www.driefleschjes.nl.
This *proeflokaal* is always pleasantly busy, with a throng of people at the bar, and walls lined with carafes of exotically named drinks like crème de roses, parfait amour and ratafia.

Wynand Fockink

Pijlsteeg 31 (near Dam square),
Oude Zijde. 020 639 2695.
www.wynand-fockink.nl.
The oldest *jenever* bar in the city, Wynand Fockink offers a wide selection of *jenever* and other fruit-based local spirits, with the opportunity to try before you buy. The place is small inside, but it's possible to stand in a covered courtyard outside year-round.

Other Cafes

Café van Daele

Paleisstraat 101. Nieuwe Zijde. 020
620 1435. www.cafevandaele.nl.
Close to Kalverstraat shops, this cafe is a welcome break after you've shopped til you are ready to drop. Split level and steeped in old-fashioned ambiance, it serves everything from mint tea and a toastie to *gluhwein* and apple tarts.

Café de Koe

Marnixstraat 381. 020 625 4482.
www.cafedekoe.nl.
A basement cafe close to the Melkweg concert and club venue, de Koe is popular with local creative types. Pop in for a beer before a gig. They serve food too, so it's a good opportunity to take the edge off your hunger.

Café Tabac

Brouwersgracht 101. Jordaan. 020 622 4413. www.cafetabac.eu

With a great location on the corner of two of Amsterdam's most prestigious canals, Tabac makes the most of its limited space. In summer, giant cushions and chairs are strewn on any available spot outside, and customers can watch boats go by.

Café ter Brugge

Overtoom 578. 020 612 9983.

Out of town compared to most of Amsterdam's cafe hot spots, Ter Brugge has an undeniably local feel. Its large terrace is packed with young professionals who live or work in the Oud-West enjoying after-office drinks. For big international football matches, it also rigs up an outdoor screen.

Café de Vergulde Gaper

Prinsenstraat 28-30. Jordaan. 020 624 8975. www.goodfoodgroup.nl

One of a small chain of recently renovated cafes (equivalent to the English gastro-pubs), Café de Vergulde Gaper now serves up food that is a notch above regular pub grub, as well as a wide selection of drinks. Also try its sister cafes, Het Molenpad and Cafe Proust.

Tearooms

Amstel Amsterdam

Professor Tulpplein 1. 020 622 6060. www.amstelamsterdam.com.

It's pricey, but high tea at this hotel is a must for an indulgent Sunday afternoon. Enjoy starched white tablecloths, more waiting staff than you need, and a different brew to go with every "course" brought on old-fashioned trolleys.

Gartine

Taksteeg 7, Nieuwe Zijde. 020 320 4132. www.gartine.nl. Reservations advised.

Tucked down a tiny alley off busy Kalverstraat, Gartine is a step into a tasteful version of your grandmother's living room. Lunch is served, but the real treat is afternoon tea, with a stack of cakes, tarts and pots of organic tea.

Tea Bar

Haarlemmerdijk 71, Jordaan. 020 623 3211. www.teabar.nl.

This modern temple to tea is more than just a cafe. It sells literally hundreds of varieties of tea and all manner of paraphernalia for the leaf. But coffee lovers need not despair: the coffee machine makes an excellent brew, and it's possible to sit and enjoy your tipple at the minimalist cafe upstairs.

Multi-tasking Cafes

Unlike many cities whose cafe culture invites you to go to one venue for coffee, another for beer, and another for a light meal, many of Amsterdam's cafes are geared to offer all three and more. Open mornings for breakfast, coffee and a selection of newspapers, many cafes transform in late afternoon into ideal spots for a beer on a sunny terrace or a glass of wine after work. Licensing laws mean that many cafes stay open until 1am, serving alcoholic drinks till late. As a result, many nightclubs don't get going until well after midnight.

ALL-STAR ARCHITECTURE

Amsterdam draws visitors from all over the world largely because of the magical atmosphere inherent in cities built beside water. Its canals are the main attraction, backed as they are by uniquely designed houses steeped in a Dutch sense of moderation. Couple those with splendid churches like the Nieuwe Kerk, grand public squares with fountains and monuments, and modern buildings such as NEMO, and the city becomes a veritable smorgasbord of architectural gems. Here are highlights embodying traditional and contemporary styles to whet your appetite for the visual feast that awaits you.

Churches

Prior to the Netherlands' mid-17C Golden Age of architecture, churches in Amsterdam were constructed in the Gothic style of the Middle Ages in the cruciform (or cross) design. **Hendrick de Keyser**, the leading artist of the Dutch Renaissance, designed three of Amsterdam's churches: the Zuiderkerk, the Westerkerk and the Noorderkerk. During the Golden Age, many of the city's Protestant churches were built in circular form, often with a dome, such as Amsterdam's Ronde Lutherse Kerk (1671).

Oude Kerk★

Oudekerksplein 23. Open Mon–Sat 11am–5pm, Sun 1pm–5pm. Closed 1 Jan, 30 Apr and 25 Dec. €5, children under 13 free; additional €7 to visit the tower Thu–Sat only. 020 625 8284. www.oudekerk.nl.
Gothic architecture did not appear in the Low Countries until the 14C. The oldest sacred building in the city is this "Old Church," begun in 1306 and altered several times. It is built in **Brabant-style Gothic**, which resembles Flamboyant Gothic. Imported as a result of the power of the Burgundians, the style is found in many buildings

Oude Kerk

©Daniel Bras/Oude Kerk

Choir screen, Nieuwe Kerk

in Belgium. Their exteriors have open-work gables and crocket spires, tall windows, flying buttresses and a tall, tiered belfry. The interiors have a slender central nave with pointed vaulting resting on round columns with crocket capitals and a triforium.

The style's influence is seen in Oude Kerk's three aisles and an ambulatory with radiating chapels. In the 16C the bell tower was crowned by an elegant spire; its carillon was cast partly by François Hemony. The massive tower forms a porch on the west side. The side chapels are topped by triangular gables. There is almost no transept. The Lady Chapel has three **stained-glass windows★**, installed in 1555. The more traditional rose window has been replaced by great bays.

Inside, the **organ loft★** above the entrance to the nave was crafted in 1724 by Jan Westerman.

Nieuwe Kerk★★

Dam square. Open daily 10am–5pm. Closed 25 Dec & 1 Jan. €5, 15 and under free. 020 638 6909. www.nieuwekerk.nl.

The Protestant New Church, which serves as the national church of the Netherlands *(see Districts)*, was constructed in the **Flamboyant Gothic** style a century after the Old Church.

Stone was rare in the Low Countries and, because the subsoil was too light to guarantee the necessary stability, the vault consists of a wooden barrel vault, like the one in the Oude Kerk. The edifice was pillaged and gutted by fire several times. After a devastating fire in 1645, the church was rebuilt in its present Gothic style; its tower remained unfinished.

Dutch and Flemish artists of the day were commissioned to embellish the church **interior**. Highlights include the **pulpit** and its magnificent sounding board, the highly ornate copper **choir screen** crafted by Johannes Lutma, the elaborately carved triptych **panel** in front of the de Ruyter monument, and the organ, which was painted by Gerrit Janszoon van Bronckhorst.

81

Westerkerk

©NBTC

Westerkerk★

Prinsengracht 281. Open Mon–Fri 11am–3pm. 020 624 7766. www.westerkerk.nl.

The Renaissance reached the Netherlands at a relatively late stage, and its pure Italian form appears hardly at all. However, Mannerism (a transitional form between Renaissance and Baroque) flourished in Holland. This Renaissance-style Western Church, built between 1620 and 1631, was designed by **Pieter de Keyser**, based on the plans of his father Hendrick, one of the leading architects of the Dutch Renaissance period. **Hendrick de Keyser** (1565-1621) was a sculptor as well as an architect. He built several churches, mainly in Amsterdam, including the Zuiderkerk and Noorderkerk. De Keyser's Mannerist style contained Baroque elements and was a forerunner of the Baroque style; his buildings were more monumental, with an imposing feeling of line. Indeed, Westerkerk is the largest Protestant church in the city.

Its **bell tower★★** rises an amazing 85m/280ft. The tower's remarkable carillon *(played Tue noon–1pm)* dates from 1638 and is the work of **François Hemony**. Atop the tower the **imperial crown** is the symbol of Maximilian I of Austria, his repayment to the city for its support of the Austro-Burgundian princes. The tower also bears Amsterdam's coat of arms. Mullions and tracery mark the windows of the nave's clerestory; small dormer windows, designed to let light into the attic, punctuate the roof.

The church **interior** is quite plain; the nave has wooden barrel vaulting and the 12 chandeliers are copies of the originals. The magnificent painted **organ panels** are the work of Gerard de Lairesse.

Canal Houses

Canal houses have a **foundation** reaching far down in the porous subsoil of the city. Long piles hewn of strong pine trunks were imported from Germany and Scandinavia, some as long as 18m/58ft. Layers of sand, peat, sand and clay, and sand and peat again composed the subsoil. Architects had to find the layer of sand in the subsoil, beginning at depth of 13m/42ft.

To reduce the risk of fire, **brick** was the construction material mandated by law. The house itself was divided into a *voorhuis* or **front house** and an *achterhuis* or **rear house**, separated by a small courtyard. The front house typically consisted of five storeys topped by a roof of pantiles. The ground floor was raised above the level of the quayside since the cellar could not be deep.

The frontage is usually narrow because rates were calculated as a function of the width.

Most frontages are three bays wide, but over time, decorative elements changed a good deal, especially gables.

A **gable** is the upper section of a frontage, set on a level with the

attic. In Amsterdam, **attics** were used as storehouses; goods were raised up into them by a **hoist** attached to the house. Since the narrow vertical structure did not cover the entire width of the rafters, the gable was flanked with a range of sandstone ornamentation, from scrolled console to ornate carved features. Below are several canal houses that exemplify various gables typical of Dutch residential architecture.

Huis aan de Drie Grachten★
Overlooking the Grimburgwal and two other canals, this house (1609) has a **stepped gable** on which the slopes have been replaced by tiers. A sandstone shelf at the top protects the structure from rain. This type of gable was used

Gables

There are countless different forms of gables. Late medieval houses were made of wood, an had simple **pointed gables (A)**. Later on, they were built with pinnacles or **crow steps (B)** *(see Huis Leeuwenburg above)*. A pitched roof was hidden behind the gable.

Later on, gables became taller, and **Dutch gables (C)** and **neck gables (D)** were used. These had triangular or curved pediments, often elaborately sculpted on either side.

The finest houses had broader façades and a roof running parallel with the street. The roof was hidden by a large pilaster gable ending in a triangular pediment or an **emblazoned balustrade crowned with statues and a coat of arms (E)**.

Finally, a large type of house developed with pilasters and a **triangular carved pediment (F)**. The façade was sometimes made of stone and decorated with garlands. The many warehouses mostly have a simple, undecorated **spout gable (G)**.

M. Guillou/MICHELIN

between 1600 and 1665, and again in the 19C when it became fashionable to build in this style.

No. 392 Herengracht

This house dates from 1665. Its **bell-shaped gable** has the characteristic shape that has given it its name. This type of gable was built between 1645 and 1790. Originally it was wide and topped by a rounded pediment; gradually its shape gained emphasis and, influenced by the Louis XV style, it lost its pediment.

No. 8 Singel

The gable on this house is a **raised neck gable** dating from the early 18C. This type of gable was built between 1640 and 1770, and gets its name from the Dutch word *halsgevel* (*hals* means "neck") because the base of the gable forms a 90-degree angle.

No. 40 Singel

Dating from 1725, this house has a **fake attic** in the ornate Louis XIV style. The original steps have disappeared, replaced by a decorative top section.

No. 237 Oudezijds Voorburgwal

The gable has disappeared on this house also. Its more sophisticated construction dates from the mid-18C: an **entablature** topped by a traceried attic with a balustrade. This type of tall construction, which was specific to the 18C, still concealed the ridge of the roof.

No. 397 Keizersgracht

This house dates to c. 1790. It has an elegantly traceried entablature and a hipped roof. In this case, the roof is visible, preventing the use of the gable. The hoist, however, is still in place. This type of construction continued to exist until about 1920.

Windmills

The earliest windmills appeared in the mid-13C. In the past, some 900 windmills ringed Amsterdam to protect it from flooding; fewer than a handful remain within the city today.

There are two types of windmills: **watermills** and **windmills**. Among these are polder mills and industrial mills. **Polder mills,**

Three "Classic" Dutchmen

The mid-17C marked a break with the graceful, ethereal style of the Renaissance. Yet Baroque architecture was so ingrained in Holland that it was described as **Dutch Classicism**, which dominated the country's Golden Age of architecture. One of the most famous architects of this age was **Jacob van Campen** (1595-1657), who designed the town hall (1648-62) that later became the royal palace. Attracted by the designs of Palladio and Mansart, he had a decisive influence on national architecture. His residential designs contain some of the finest examples of Dutch Classicism. **Philip Vingboons** (1607-78) was the best known exponent of the style. He designed a reserved form of architecture, a kind of sober luxury that met the demands of a Protestant clientele. The most austere example was the work of another great architect, **Adriaan Dortsman** (1625-82), who trained as a mathematician and designed the Nieuwe Lutherse Kerk (1671) on the Singel.

perched along dikes overlooking the **polders** (reclaimed land that must be routinely drained) were used to pump water; industrial mills were used to grind corn, extract oil, saw timber. **Smock mills** are most commonly seen in the north. They stand on a brick base. The topmost section (the cap) rotates to turn into the wind.

Sloten Windmill
In Sloten. Akersluis 10. Open daily 10am–4:30pm. Closed 1 Jan, 30 Apr, 25-26 Dec. 020 669 0412. www.molenvansloten.nl.
On the outskirts of Amsterdam, in Sloten, stands the **Molen van Sloten**. It was reconstructed from the body of a mid-19C windmill that was moved here from eastern Amsterdam in 1991.

The windmill is an example of a **smock mill**, used to draw up water. It operates on the principle of the worm screw. The **screw** (or jack) can be seen, linked to pinions to the central pivot that activates the sails by means of the **toothed cylinder**. On the gallery are the **fantail** and the tall pole used to move the cap. In this position the miller can use a rope to activate the brake control lever that blocks all four arms, so that he can mount or remove the sails.
Visitors can take a tour that explains how the windmill works.

De Gooyer Windmill
Not open to the public. Next door to Brouwerij 't IJ brewpub at Funenkade 7.
Nestled between the Kadijken and the Eastern Docklands is Molen De Gooyer, a so-called **platform windmill**, which is operated from a raised platform that encircles the

De Gooyer Windmill

© Photolibrary / age fotostock

entire structure.
From the 17C to the 19C, a number of flour mills were located on the city's defensive walls, all of which were demolished save for De Gooyer. The windmill was moved several times from this site until it was finally returned here in 1814, atop a new stone base, and eventually restored.

Adjacent, in a former bathhouse, local microbrewery Brouwerij 't IJ turns out 250,000 liters of beer per year, much of which is served in their on-site pub.

Military Architecture
The development of longer-range artillery meant that fortifications had to be constructed at increasing distances from the towns they were built to defend. Forts were erected in a circle around the towns, and in places that could not be flooded. The circle of some 45 forts that form the **Amsterdam Citadel** is an average of 12km/7.4mi from the capital; one is the island fort

of **Pampus** in the IJsselmeer. This famous defense line, built between 1883 and 1920, has been a **UNESCO World Heritage Site** since 1996. The earlier citadel of **Den Helder** was built by Napoleon in 1811.

Modern Architecture

In the early 19C, architects again sought their inspiration in the past; first from ancient Greece and Rome (**Neoclassicism**), and later the Middle Ages and Renaissance (**neo-Gothic** and **neo-Renaissance**). In **Eclecticism**, these stylistic elements were used together. One of the most important architects in this period, **Petrus Josephus Cuypers** (1827-1921), introduced a form of neo-Gothic to his buildings, which included Amsterdam's Rijksmuseum and the central railway station. Although architecture of earlier eras was a major source of inspiration for the 19C, it was also in this period that new materials such as **cast iron** and **steel** were first used. During the 20C and 21C, architecture experienced, and continues to experience, something of a renaissance in the Netherlands. Amsterdam has several examples.

Centraal Station
Stationsplein. Open 24hrs daily.
The huge central station on three artificial islands in the River IJ aroused great controversy when it was built between 1881 and 1889, mainly because it blocked the view of the port. The gigantic building is a **Neo-Renaissance** construction designed by **P.J.H. Cuypers** (*above*) and **A.L. van Gendt** (1835-1901). It took seven

years to build it on 8,700 piles. The red and white brick façade visible from Damrak is one of the city's best-known buildings and serves as an orientation point. It features two square towers bearing a clock (*right*) and a weathervane (*left*).

Rijksmuseum★★★
Jan Luijkenstraat 1. Open daily 9am–6pm. Closed 1 Jan. €12.50; 18 and under free. 020 674 7000. www.rijksmuseum.nl.
This vast temple to art was designed by **P.J.H. Cuypers**, whose plans won first prize in a government competition in 1875. The monumental red-brick building, completed in a predominantly Neo-Gothic style in 1885, is distinguished by its turrets and extensive façade ornamentation. The theme of the decorative features is the role of the Netherlands in the history of fine arts. Sculptors Bart van Hove and François Vermeylen produced the detailed work. The likeness of Rembrandt is represented several times and in life-size carvings. The museum is undergoing major renovation slated for completion in 2013.

Van Gogh Museum★★★
Paulus Potterstraat 7. Open daily 10am–6pm, Fri 10am–10pm. Closed 1 Jan. €14, under 18 free. 020 570 5200. www.vangoghmuseum.nl.
Opened in 1973, the museum building embodies the trends introduced by the De Stijl ("the style") movement (*see sidebar below*). The singular concept behind the movement's designs was that only mathematical structures could express the true

essence of things. The architect, **Gerrit Rietveld** (1888-1964), was one of De Stijl's leading personalities.

His greatest work was the Schröder House (1924) in Utrecht, a concrete construction of juxtaposed cubes. The same principle is recognizable in the Van Gogh Museum, but it has been adapted to suit the use of the building as a museum. Visitors are amazed at the light pouring into a building that looks from the outside like a totally enclosed block of concrete.

Beurs van Berlage★
Damrak 277. Hours vary by event. Cafe open Mon–Sat 10am–6pm, Sun 11am–6pm. 020 530 4141. www.beursvanberlage.nl.
Architect **H.P. Berlage** (1856–1934) built the eponymous Beurs van Berlage, completed in 1903. It originally served as the Stock Exchange, but is now a popular convention center. When it was finished, the Beurs van Berlage ushered in a new era of architecture. Berlage was the precursor of Rationalism, an architectural movement that placed emphasis on simplicity of line and the rational use of building materials. Although inspired by Romanesque architecture, the building marked a profound change. Form met the requirements of certain precise functions and the utilitarian elements were clearly highlighted, resulting in unusual decoration such as the structures bolted onto the roof.

Algemene Bank Nederland
Vijzelstraat 32. City Archives open Tues–Fri 10am–5pm, Sat–Sun 11am–5pm. 020 251 1510. www.stadsarchief.amsterdam.nl.
K.P.C. de Bazel (1869–1923) applied the same concepts of the Amsterdam School to his design of this Amsterdam bank. He worked in a way similar to Berlage, emphasizing the building's materials and function. No longer a bank, the building now houses the Amsterdam City Archives.

Amsterdam School and De Stijl

A group of architects influenced by **Hendrik Petrus Berlage** (*see Stock Exchange*) formed the **Amsterdam School** (c. 1912–23), which strove for a less austere architecture than that of Berlage. Leading members of this movement included **Michel de Klerk, Piet L. Kramer** and **Johan Melchior van der Mey**. They were the great masters of urban renewal; their work made expressionistic use of brick. Influenced by Frank Lloyd Wright, **W.M. Dudok** stood slightly apart from the Amsterdam School. At the same time, the **De Stijl** movement was being founded by painters **Piet Mondrian** and **Theo van Doesburg** and architect **J.J.P. Oud**. Architects such as **Gerrit Rietveld**, who designed the Van Gogh Museum, **J. Duiker** and **B. Bijvoet** also gained their inspiration from the movement, using concrete skeletons and superimposing and juxtaposing cube-shaped spaces to form a whole. This process was known as **Nieuwe Bouwen** (New Building) or **Functionalism**, which was at its height from 1920-1940.

A Peek Behind the Scenes

Since 1987, nationwide **Open Monument Day** (*Open Monumentendag*) has offered an insider's look at private residences and courtyards, businesses and warehouses, churches and other monuments in Amsterdam and other Dutch cities, as part of the European Heritage Days. Each year, on the second weekend in September, 60-odd monuments in Amsterdam open their doors to the public (a considerable number are closed the rest of the year); others allow visitors into rooms that are normally cordoned off. Organized on a theme, such as 2010's "Taste of the 19C" or 2011's "New Use, Old Building," the event is broadened by exhibits, lectures, tours and other activities that complement the theme. There is no charge to visit, but due to space limitations, some monuments and activities require advance reservations. Not all monuments are open both days, so check the website (www.amsterdam. nl/openmonumentendag) or brochure for the hours.

NEMO★

Oosterdok 2. Open Tue–Sun (Jun–Aug and school holidays daily) 10am–5pm. Closed 1 Jan, 30 Apr and 25 Dec. €12.50, children 3 and under free. 020 531 3233. www.e-nemo.nl.

Opened in 1997 this science and technology center *(see For Kids)* was conceived by the Italian architect **Renzo Piano**, designer of the Centre Pompidou in Paris (along with Rogers). Its massive green shape resembles a ship ready to launch; the enormous hull faces in the direction of the IJ River. Built over the IJ Tunnel, the huge structure relies on the tunnel for its foundation. Clad in copper—a material that enables the curved-shaped structure to flex—the building must move to counter the weight of traffic in the tunnel below.

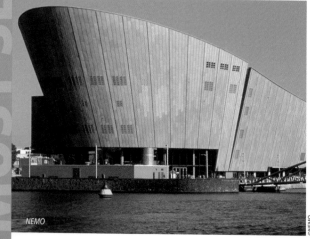

NEMO

©NEMO

MUST SEE

The five-floor interior is divided into six sections called "districts." The architect's deliberate design of the building without a lot of windows helps keep visitors focused on the exhibits inside. Piano left the pipes and wiring visible to convey his sense of the interior as a "factory."

He wished to give the city an elevated observation point, so he designed a **roof terrace**, the highest in the city. To take advantage of the **view★★**, use the upper entrance, via the long ramp that runs from the road tunnel under the IJ River.

ARCAM

Prins Hendrikkade 600. Open Tue–Fri 1pm–5pm. 020 620 4878. www.arcam.nl.
ARCAM, or the Architecture Center Amsterdam, is a repository of the city's architectural history. It's only fair that the design of its headquarters should be on a par with some of the city's most extraordinary structures. "Sculptural" is a word often used to describe the boldly curvaceous form of this diminutive space by architect **René van Zuuk**. While the waterfront side is a patchwork of windows, the back and sides of the building are enrobed in zinc-coated aluminum that makes for an overall streamlined effect.

Inside, the different sections of the airy space flow effortlessly into one another to give the same sense of freedom reflected in the exterior's contours.

Visitors are invited to explore the center and its exhibits at no admission cost.

Architecture Tours and Routes

Learn more about the city's architecture by way of recommended routes and expert-led tours. **ARCAM** (*see above*) has the broadest selection of architectural routes for tourists: in addition to their architectural maps of different city districts, their handy **Archishuttle** series allows commuters to turn their tram ride into an informative tour, with a rundown of the star architecture visible on four different tram lines. ARCAM also offers a GPS hand-held device that steers visitors on a course of the city's architectural points of interest. The **City Walks Office** (*Stadswandelkantoor; www.stadswandelkantoor.nl*) provides a variety of themed tours; visitors can take in architecture old or new, in the center or the outskirts, on foot or by bike (provided by the tour company).

Some museums offer docent-led tours: **Museum Amsterdam Noord** leads visitors around its namesake district to view wooden houses and bold new structures; **Museum Het Schip** focuses its tours on the architecture of the 19C Amsterdam School of Michel de Klerk and his contemporaries; and the **Van Eesterenmuseum** (*Burgemeester de Vlugtlaan 125; open Fri–Sat 11am–5pm; €5, children 12 and under free; 020 447 1857; www.vaneesterenmuseum.nl*) explores urban architecture and development, such as that associated with city architect Cornelis van Eesteren, in its 2pm tours, included in the museum admission fee.

OLD MASTERS ON VIEW

Ask any world traveler to name a museum in Amsterdam and it's very likely that the reply will be the Rijksmuseum or the Van Gogh Museum—or both. That's how world famous these museums are. Along with the city's ode to modern art, the Stedelijk Museum, these three heavyweights reside in what is termed Amsterdam's Museum Quarter, located southwest of city center and just below the Singelgracht and the Leidseplein area. They occupy a vast green expanse with a lengthy reflecting pool that is called the Museumplein, which culminates in the Concertgebouw at the southern end.

Rijksmuseum★★★

Jan Luijkenstraat 1. Open daily 9am–6pm. Closed 1 Jan. €12.50, 18 and under free. 020 674 7000. www.rijksmuseum.nl. Open during renovation period.

This famous national museum (literally the "state museum") is best known for its exceptional collection of 15C–17C **Dutch art**, including magnificent works by well-known Dutch masters **Rembrandt van Rijn**, **Johannes Vermeer** and **Frans Hals**. The collections of sculpture and decorative arts, Dutch history, prints, Asiatic art, costumes and textiles are also impressive. In 1808 Louis Napoleon, the

brother of Napoleon, signed a decree ordering the founding of a great national museum. He decided to transfer the collection of 225 paintings the French set up at The Hague in 1798.

Two buildings successively housed the collection before the present neo-Gothic style building was completed by P.J.H. Cuypers in in1885.

A major restoration of the main building is currently underway; completion is expected by 2013. During this time, the Rijksmuseum is displaying only the best of its permanent collection in an exhibit entitled *The Masterpieces* in the Philips Wing. *Not all of the paintings mentioned are on view.*

Detail of The Night watch *(1642) by Rembrandt van Rijn*

Detail of The Windmill at Wijk bij Duurstede *(1670) by Jacob van Ruysdael*

©Rijksmuseum

Dutch Paintings★★★
(15C–17C)

The collection of **pre-Renaissance** paintings includes works by **Geertgen tot Sint-Jans**, such as his *Adoration of the Magi,* and Jan Mostaert, whose painting of the same subject is set amid an Italian Renaissance scene.

In the **Renaissance** section, **Lucas van Leyden's** *Adoration of the Golden Calf* shows great mastery of composition; **Jan van Scorel** depicts a *Mary Magdalene* of very Italian elegance. Both Cornelis Corneliszoon van Haarlem and Abraham Bloemaert are representatives of **Mannerism**.

In the **Golden Age**, painting styles varied a great deal. Hendrick Avercamp specialized in winter scenes, such as *Winter Landscape.* **Frans Hals'** outstanding portraits include *Isaac Massa and his Wife,* while his vivid brushwork of *The Jolly Drinker* is reminiscent of Impressionism. **Jan Steen's** trademark was cheerful domestic scenes (*The Feast of St. Nicholas, Woman at her Toilet*).

Other leading landscape artists included **Jacob van Ruysdael** (*The Windmill at Wijk bij Duurstede,* and *View of Haarlem*). Adriaen van Ostade was more interested

Touring Tip

Despite its renovation, 400 of the Rijksmuseum's most cherished 17C masterpieces remain on view, in addition to the several temporary exhibits it continues to hold each year. Allow at least 90min to 2hrs to see it all. Themed audio tours can be rented for €5 a piece; one tour offers visitors a deeper acquaintance with 30 of the "Masterpieces" on exhibit, while another, developed for children from 6 to 12 years of age, explores 17C food and drink, a popular subject for the Dutch masters. Because there is often a substantial wait at the ticket counter, advance e-tickets are recommended; these can be purchased via the Rijksmuseum website.

OLD MASTERS

in villagers and their daily lives (*Peasants in an Interior: The Skaters*). The four works by **Vermeer** are all masterpieces: *The Little Street* (c. 1658), painted from the windows of his house; *The Milkmaid* (c. 1660), pouring milk with a measured gesture; *Woman in Blue Reading a Letter* (c. 1662), in luminous blue tones; and finally *The Love Letter* (c. 1666).

The best-known work on view by **Rembrandt** is his painting **The Night Watch**. Commissioned by a company of the civic guard, this enormous group portrait was completed in 1642. It owes its name to the darkened varnish, which was cleaned in 1947, but the painting in fact depicts the company in broad daylight. Paintings from the **Italian School** include Primitives, such as a remarkable *Madonna of the Lily* by Fra Angelico. Two works by **Peter**

Paul Rubens are among the Flemish paintings.

Major paintings by Dutch masters from the latter 17C include late works by Rembrandt: *Portrait of Titus in a Monk's Habit* (1600); *Self-Portrait as the Apostle Paul* (1661) showing Rembrandt as a disillusioned old man; *The Syndics*, a masterpiece dating from 1662 showing inspectors of the Drapers' Guild grouped behind a table with a red tablecloth.

Old Woman at Prayer is a work by Nicolaes Maes, a contemporary of Rembrandt. **Albert Cuyp** was a versatile landscape painter whose compositions featured shepherds, cattle and small human figures.

Sculpture and Decorative Arts★★★

The museum has a rich collection of furniture and works of art from the 15C to the 20C. Among the sculpture from the Low Countries are **bronze statuettes** (Brabant, 1476) used to decorate the tomb of Isabella de Bourbon.

The **Annunciation of the Virgin Mary** by German sculptor **Tilman Riemenschneider** is typically late Gothic, while the 16C Brussels wall tapestry *The Triumph of Fame over Death* shows the influence of the Italian Renaissance.

The **treasury** contains fine goblets, bowls, dishes and jewelry. Note the map of the Iberian Peninsula, the **chess set**, a Colonial ebony bed, delftware and a lacquer cabinet. Of particular interest are finely detailed **dollhouses**, 18C canopy beds, a 1730 **apothecary's chest**, Meissen porcelain, and enamelled snuffboxes.

Dutch History★★

Art is used to retrace the history of the Netherlands from the Eighty Years' War through to World War II. The **VOC-Galerij** tells the story of the East India Company through the eyes of the men who sailed its ships. The huge painting, *The Battle of Waterloo, 18 June 1815* by J.W. Pieneman, recalls the victory over Napoleon. The chair used by William III at his inauguration in the Nieuwe Kerk in 1849 is on display.

Prints Room★★
(Rijksprentenkabinet)

The museum possesses more than a million drawings and engravings from the 15C to the present day, including the largest collection of etchings by **Rembrandt**.

Dutch Paintings★ (18C–19C)

Paintings in the 18C were hung at the time in rows, one above the other, as the work, *The Gallery of Brentano in his house on Herengracht*, by Adriaan de Lelie illustrates. The rooms dedicated to the 19C include the Napoleonic

©Rijksmuseum

Doll's house, Petronella Oortmans (1647)

era (P.G. van Os), and Dutch Romanticism (Barend C. Koekkoek; W.J.J. Nuyen's *Shipwreck on a Rocky Coast*). George Breitner and Jacobus van Looy (*Summer Luxury*) are important representatives of Amsterdam Impressionism.

Costumes and Textiles

A changing selection of items from the collection are usually displayed, including 18C and 19C Dutch costumes, oriental carpets, lace and linen damask.

Museum Deals

Amsterdam's world-renowned museums don't come cheap. With admission fees at €10 or more, the costs can add up for visitors who hope to see several museums on their trip. Fortunately, several discount cards allow tourists to experience more for less. The most popular choice is the **I amsterdam City Card**, which includes free admission to more than 50 museums as well as 60 discount offers; cards are available for 24-, 48- or 72-hour periods (at €39, €49 and €59, respectively) from the Amsterdam Tourism and Convention Board (www.iamsterdam.com). The **Holland Pass** (www.hollandpass.com) offers free or discounted admission and fast-track entry (where applicable) to 2 to 7 attractions in several major Dutch cities, as well as free public transport and special offers. For visitors on an extended stay, the **Museumkaart** (Museum Card, www.museumkaart.nl), at €39.95 for adults and €19.95 for those under 18 years, is an unbeatable deal for a year's worth of free admission to more than 400 museums nationwide.

Asiatic Art★

A changing selection of some 500 objects from the Indian subcontinent, Cambodia, Indonesia, Japan and China is usually on display. The 12C bronze, *Shiva, Lord of the Dance*, represents India. The small sculptured 7C or 8C *Buddha Shakyamuni* is from Indonesia. Chinese sculptures include an elegant seated Buddha. The Japanese collection includes ceramics for the tea ceremony, lacquer items and delicately painted screens.

Van Gogh Museum★★★

Paulus Potterstraat 7. Open daily 10am–6pm (Fri til 10pm). Closed 1 Jan. €14, under 18 free. 020 570 5200. www.vangoghmuseum.nl.

This museum is home to the world's largest collection of works by renowned Dutch painter **Vincent Van Gogh** (1853–90), who was born in Noord-Brabant. It holds more than 200 **paintings** and some 600 **drawings** by the artist, as well as the **letters** he wrote to his brother Theo. The painting collection traces the artist's development from the somber canvases of his early career to the violent tonalities of his last years. **Works by contemporaries** of Van Gogh such as Toulouse-Lautrec, Gauguin, Chaval and Redon are also on display.

Designed by the architect **Gerrit Rietveld**, the main museum building opened in 1973. The Exhibition Wing, a separate oval pavilion behind the museum, was designed by **Kisho Kurokawa** and opened in 1999; here, temporary exhibits of late-19C art seek to give greater insight into the world of art of Van Gogh's time *(take the underground walkway from the main galleries to get to the wing).* On **Friday nights**, the museum becomes a popular meeting spot, with a bar, DJ, video projections and comfortable chairs.

Renovation of the museum is expected to begin in 2012. During the process approximately 75 paintings as well as works on paper by Van Gogh will be on display at the Hermitage Amsterdam museum as of October 2012.

Since the collection is rotated, not all paintings described below may be on view.

Van Gogh Museum, with Exhibition Wing in foreground

©Jannes Linders/Van Gogh Musuem

Detail of Portrait of Vincent Van Gogh Painting Sunflowers *(1888) by Paul Gauguin*

©Van Gogh Museum

Nuenen Period
(December 1883-November 1885)

Dark hues dominated Van Gogh's large drawings and watercolors during this period; he depicted the misery that surrounded him. **The Potato Eaters** (1885) linked the artist to the great Realist traditions of Dutch painting through subject matter and through the brutal contrasts in the chiaroscuro. His father died in March of 1885; Van Gogh travelled to Antwerp and from there, to Paris in 1886 to join his brother Theo, who managed a gallery in Montmartre.

Paris Period
(February 1886-February 1888)

In Antwerp he attended classes at the town's academy of art and saw his first Japanese prints. Van Gogh returned to Paris and discovered the Impressionists, becoming friends with Toulouse-Lautrec and others. His style underwent a profound change: he used lighter colors and his compositions rapidly became less tortured. Because he couldn't afford models, he used his own image, marking the beginning of a long series of self-portraits. Most of the portraits in the museum were painted in Paris. **Self-Portrait in front of an Easel** (1888) and **Self-Portrait in a Grey Hat** (1887) are among his most introspective works. An oil on cardboard, his **Self-Portrait in a Straw Hat** (1887) shows his increasing frequent visits to the country to escape the noise of Paris. Done in the same year, *Cornfield with a Lark* and *Woodland* are forerunners of future works painted in the open air.

His still-lifes evolved from painting flowers given to him by friends to works with fruit, most importantly **Apples, Grapes, Lemons and Pears** (1887).

Arles Period
(February 1888-May 1889)

Influenced by the southern sunshine, Van Gogh began using more luminous colors; his paintings acquired a new chromatic power—and a serenity.

He painted countless landscapes, several in the style of Japanese prints, such as **Fishing Boats on the Beach at Les Saintes-Maries-de-la-Mer** (1888). Seeing a work by Millet, he painted the small but outstanding **The Sower** (1888). The next year he completed **The Sunflowers**, which, to him, symbolized gratitude.

Saint-Remy Period

(May 1889-May 1890) Having cut off his ear and been hospitalized, he suffered increasingly violent hallucinations and entered an asylum of his own accord. There he continued to paint. In the artist's painting **Cornfield with Reaper** (1889), he saw the figure as Death and the corn as humanity being cut down. Though reminiscent of the Arles period in its coloring, **The Irises** (1890) is an expression of his internal torment.

Auvers-sur-Oise

(May 1890-July 29, 1890) In May he travelled north of Paris to **Auvers-sur-Oise** to receive treatment from Dr. Gachet.

The final paintings include **The Château d'Auvers** (1890), with its melancholy atmosphere; **Tree Roots** (1890), with a twisted composition close to abstraction; **Cornfield under a Stormy Sky** (1890), outstanding for the depth of the large expanses of two colors; and **Cornfield with Crows** (1890), a highly dramatic work. Overwhelmed by his feeling of mental isolation and convinced he was going insane, Van Gogh shot himself through the heart and died two days later, with his brother Theo at his bedside.

Works by Contemporaries

Among the paintings of Van Gogh's fellow artists on view are *Tulip Fields and Mills near Leyden* (1886) by Claude Monet; **Young Woman at a Table** (1887) by Henri de Toulouse-Lautrec; and **Portrait of Vincent Van Gogh Painting Sunflowers** (1888) by Paul Gauguin. Other noteworthy works include **The Boat** (1897) by Odilon Redon, *Rue de l'Epicerie, Rouen* (1898) by Camille Pissaro and **Still Life with Flowers** (c 1901) by Pablo Picasso.

Stedelijk Museum★★★

Paulus Potterstraat 13 (temporary entrance while museum is under renovation); Museumplein 10 (post-renovation). Open Tue–Sun 10am–5pm (Thu til 10pm). €10, children 13–18 €5, under 13 free. 020 523 1822. www.stedelijk.nl.

Befitting a musem of modern art, the Stedelijk is getting a radical facelift. Its exterior will definitely attract attention—and already has. Completed in 1895, 10 years later than the Rijksmuseum, the original

Sunflowers
(1888) by Vincent Van Gogh

©Van Gogh Museum

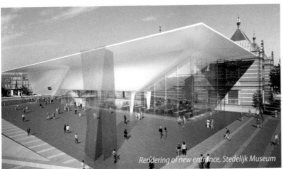

Rendering of new entrance, Stedelijk Museum
©ATCB

brick and stone building was designed in the neo-Renaissance style by A.W. Weissman (1858-1923), the municipal archtect. It was enlarged in 1954 by a wing consisting of bay windows. Currently a striking extension, known as the **The Bathtub**, is nearing completion. Designed by Amsterdam-based firm **Benthem Crouwel Architekten**, the roof-dominated façade covers an area of some 3,000sq m/32,292ft. Made of reinforced fiber, the transparent-white construction juts out over what now is the main museum entrance, which was moved to the park-like Museumplein. The new addition will include a museum shop, information center, library and terraced restaurant. A spacious exhibition hall will spread out below ground.

The Collections

Since it first opened its doors to the public in 1895, the municipal museum has been collecting works of contemporary art, and organizing exhibits from 1850 to the present. The varied collection it has amassed covers the period from 1850 to today. Paintings, sculpture, drawings and prints,

applied art and industrial design, posters, photographs and video are among the more than 90,000 works in the collection. There are works by artists who have now become a traditional part of modern art, such as Manet, Mondrian and Picasso. There are paintings by Cézanne, Kandinsky, Malevitch, Chagall, De Kooning and Lichtenstein. Recent trends in European and American art are also well represented.

Like its neighbor, the Rijksmuseum, the Stedelijk is now also drastically reduced to just a few limited exhibits in its historic quarters on Paulus Potterstraat; the reopening of this recently renovated wing is meant to hold art lovers over until the brand-new extension of the Stedelijk, which faces the Museumplein, is unveiled.

Museum History

The museum was originally founded thanks to a legacy from Sophia Augusta de Bruyn, whose husband, Lopez Suasso, had bequeathed his property to the city. Originally the municipal museum contained the collection of the Sophia-Augusta Foundation and a collection of modern art

97

Stedelijk Museum

©ATCB

consisting of 19C works. It is this latter collection that provided the works by French artists and others by The Hague School. The collection was then constantly extended and the distinction between the two collections was dropped.

Yet it was **Willem Sandberg**, curator from 1945 to 1962, who made the museum world famous. Under his leadership, it abandoned old-fashioned layouts and launched a program of international exhibitions. His purchasing policy was particularly enlightened, as is obvious from his acquisitions of works by the CoBrA group, by German Expressionists and by Russian artist Kasimir Malevich. His actions were continued by successive curators. One of the great attractions of the museum is the large number and quality of its **temporary exhibitions**, which always reflect new and emerging trends in contemporary art. Excellent examples from the past include the CoBrA group in 1949, American

Pop Art in 1964, and Nam June Paik's video art in 1976.

Collection Highlights

The museum has some 30 canvases by George Hendrik Breitner, who at the end of the 19C, was much better known in Amsterdam than Vincent Van Gogh. Note too the works by Isaac Israëls (*The Sand Dealer*, c1895) and Jacob Maris (*Polders after the Rain*, 1892), as well as Van Gogh. Early 20C Dutch artists are well represented, such as Kees van Dongen (*Old Clown*, 1910) and De Stijl's Piet Mondrian (*Tableau III, Composition dans l'ovale*, 1914). As well as many early 20C canvases by major French artists such as Braque, Bonnard and Vuillard, the museum possesses several works by German Expressionists like Franz Marc's **Blue Ponies** (1912). The 29 paintings, 7 gouaches, 15 drawings and 17 diagrams purchased in 1958 constitute a unique collection of works by Russian **Kasimir Malevich**. Henri Matisse's masterpiece **La Perruche**

et la sirène (1952) consists of paper cut-outs. The museum boasts an admirable collection of works by the **CoBrA group** *(see Museums)*, a movement whose greatest national exponent was muralist **Karel Appel**. Dutchmen Jan Schoonhoven, Ad Dekkers and Wessel Couzijn are also represented in the collections. The museum's most outstanding collection, however, is the assemblage of **American Abstract Expressionists**, including works by Willem de Kooning, Barnett Newman (*Cathedra,* 1951), Ellsworth Kelly, Kenneth Noland and others.

Museum het Rembrandthuis★

Jodenbreestraat 4. Open daily 10am–5pm. Closed 1 Jan. €10, children 6-17 €3, under 6 free. 020 520 0400. www.rembrandthuis.nl.

Take a peek into the daily life of **Rembrandt van Rijn** (1606-69) at the Rembrandt House Museum, where the artist lived for nearly two decades (1639-58). By the time, in 1639, the artist purchased the 1606 house, it had lost its original double-stepped gable. **Jacob van Campen**, the future architect of the royal palace, had altered the front just before 1630 by adding an extra storey and a triangular pediment at the top. Rembrandt, who moved from Leiden to Amsterdam in 1631, painted most of his greatest masterpieces in this house. He paid 13,000 florins for it, payable over six years. In 1658 the house had to be sold to reimburse his creditors. Amsterdam's city council stepped in to purchase the dwelling in 1906, and had it restored. It was

opened to the public as a museum in 1911. Historical documents— such as an exhaustive inventory of Rembrandt's possessions that was compiled upon his bankruptcy— allowed experts to reconstruct the home's interior with remarkable accuracy, to reflect the house as it was when Rembrandt inhabited it. Besides viewing the artist's daily environment, visitors will discover another lesser-known facet of this Dutch master: Rembrandt wasn't just a celebrated painter, he was also a prolific etcher, and the museum's collection houses a wide variety of his virtuoso prints. Works from Rembrandt's predecessors, the "Pre-Rembrandtists," his teacher and his contemporaries and pupils round out this unparalleled collection. Highlights of his etchings on view include **The Three Crosses** (c.1660), **Self-portrait with a Surprised Expression** (c.1630), **Woman with an Arrow** (c.1661), as well as his engraving called **The Three Trees** (1643).

©NBTC

Museum het Rembrandthuis

MUSEUMS IN THE MIX

The city's repositories aren't confined to the Museum Quarter alone. First-rate museums are to be found on many of Amsterdam's major canals, several situated within the monumental walls of former canal houses that have been transformed into museums for the public: such is the history of Het Grachtenhuis, dedicated to Amsterdam's UNESCO-listed canals, and the Hermitage Amsterdam, the Dutch branch of its lauded Russian counterpart. Other museums, such as the Cobra Museum for Modern Art in nearby Amstelveen, attest to the Netherlands' continued architectural prowess, with unique collections housed in remarkable new spaces.

Amsterdam Museum★★

Access via Kalverstraat 92, Sint-Luciënsteeg 27, Nieuwezijds Voorburgwal 357 or Begijnensloot (Gallery of the Civic Guards). Open Mon–Fri 10am–5pm, Sat–Sun and public holidays 11am–5pm. Closed 1 Jan, 30 Apr and 25 Dec. €10, children 6-18 years €5, under 6 free. 020 523 1822. www.amsterdammuseum.nl.

Amsterdam's history museum has been laid out within a 15C orphanage. Its exhibits tell the story of the city in a thematic chronological presentation displayed in the many rooms of a building that has often been extended, in particular by **Pieter** and **Hendrick de Keyser** and **Jacob van Campen**.

Touring Tip

The Sint-Luciënsteeg or Begijnensloot entrance is preferable, since both of them provide the opportunity to see **façade stones** from old houses that have been mounted on a wall in Sint-Luciënsteeg and the Gallery of the Civic Guard opening onto the [Gedempte] Begijnensloot.

Left of the entrance in Kalverstraat is the former boys' playground; the cubbyholes where they used to keep their belongings are in the east wing. Opposite, a building in the Classical style hosts temporary exhibits. In **Sint-Luciënsteeg** a small gateway is topped by the city's coat of arms. On one wall is a large collection of picturesque **façade-stones**. There is also a free **gallery of schutterstukken★**, group portraits of companies of the civic guard.

The Sint-Luciënsteeg entrance to the museum is through the second courtyard, formerly reserved for female orphans. Male orphans used the Kalverstraat entrance. *Follow the rooms in numerical order; they are spread over several floors. Below are highlights. An illuminated map shows the city's expansion.*

Gallery of the Civic Guard

A stroll through this room is an opportunity to understand the purpose of a painting representing the bourgeois militia, as does **Rembrandt's** *The Night Watch* (in the Rijksmuseum). Be sure to compare the *Banquet of Militiamen of the Company of Captain Jacob Backer* (1632) by Nicolaes Pickenoy with Frans Hals' *Banquet of the*

City History in a Nutshell

Amsterdam was built on sand, erected a town hall, and fairly rapidly began to trade with the rest of the world. In 1345 a miracle made it a center of pilgrimage, and then Amsterdam was subjected to Spanish rule. During this period it began to extend its influence around the world. Merchandise from ships of the **Dutch East India Company** and other companies flooded the city. At its peak the city built a new town hall, the present Royal Palace, and began attracting many artists (Rembrandt came to live here in 1630), who were commissioned by rich merchants to paint portraits and landscapes. Large numbers of buildings were constructed, including several churches. Although the town had become wealthy, it did not forget those living in poverty: charitable institutions abounded, and their regents, or governors, liked having their portraits painted. In the 18C, despite strong competition from foreign countries, Amsterdam still occupied a prominent position in the world of the arts. In 1795 the French arrived; the towns lost their independence but the country was unified. At the end of the 19C, Amsterdam experienced something of a population explosion. New developments sprang up, including the Rijksmuseum. After the horrors of World War II, Amsterdam went back to being the dynamic city it had once been, and it has remained so ever since.

Officers of the Saint-George Civic Guard, painted 16 years earlier.

Sculptures and Paintings

The fine **four oak sculptures**, including one of Wilhelm VI of Bavaria, Count of Holland, were carved by an unknown artist. There are also anonymous portraits of William of Orange and the Duke of Alba. The oldest map of Amsterdam is on view, commissioned by the city's governor c.1538, from Cornelis Anthonisz. **The Archers of the Civic Guard** (1562), by Dirck Barendsz, depicts 14 members of the G company. Don't miss Rembrandt's **Dr. Deijman's Anatomy Lesson** (1656) and the **Flower Market** (1673) by Gerri Berckheide, which illustrates a market once held on Nieuwezijds Voorburgwal.

©Monique Vermeulen/Amsterdam Museum

Courtyard, Amsterdam Museum

MUSEUMS IN THE MIX

Amsterdam Museum

©Monique Vermeulen/Amsterdam Museum

exhibits capture the prosperity of the Golden Age and show the dynamic approach to trade that the Netherlands still manifests today.

17C Regents' Room

As you leave, visit the restored chamber where the directors of the orphanage met (*to the left of the entrance*). Its marble pavement is an example of a luxurious 17C interior.

Hermitage Amsterdam★★

Amstel 51. Open daily 10am–5pm (Wed til 8pm). Closed 1 Jan, 30 Apr and 25 Dec. €15, under 17 free. 020 530 7488. www.hermitage.nl.

First a merchant's canal-side mansion, then a home for the elderly, the monumental **Amstelhof** is now the location of the Amsterdam branch of the **Hermitage Museum in St. Petersburg, Russia**. The vast space and its minimalistic interior are the perfect foil for the museum's world-class exhibits, which are as indepth as they are diverse. From Greek antiquity to Modernist art, the Hermitage's masterfully curated exhibits fill the spacious halls with precious artifacts that visitors crowd around in curiosity.

Background

The Amstelhof was first known as the Deanery; it was constructed with a fortune left by a wealthy merchant in 1680. For some 324 years, the structure provided a home to the elderly. Behind its lengthy Classical façade stretching along the Amstel River are a large courtyard, separate

Navigation and Trade

The IJ by Hendrick Cornelisz Vroom pictures an estuary that disappeared with Centraal Station's construction in 1889. Several

Yearly Museum Events

The Netherlands is certainly fond of its museums, and two annual events celebrate these cultural institutions. Each year, on the first weekend in April, museum visitors turn out in droves for **Museum Weekend** (*www.museumweekend.nl*), a nationwide event during which some 500 museums open their doors to the public for a weekend of free or discounted admission. In recent years, the event has attracted nearly one million participants. On the first Saturday of each November, **Museum Night** (*www.n8.nl*) allows art lovers to museum-hop among more than 40 institutions until 2am; special exhibits, live music and performances, films, food and drink are part of the event.

©Roos Aldershoff/State Hermitage Museum St. Petersburg

Church Hall, Hermitage Amsterdam

wings, a church hall once used as a refectory, and boardrooms where the governors met. Housing for married couples was built beside the Deanery in 1888 and called Neerlandia. Over the years there was much renovation and reconstruction until a major overhaul took place in the 1970s, when the building was thoroughly modernized.

Museum's Debut

In 2004 the Neerlandia building was renovated as a museum where exhibits from the prestigious collection of Russia's Hermitage Museum were displayed. Following a two-year conversion, the entire Amstelhof complex was reopened—amid great fanfare and fireworks—in mid-2009 as the Hermitage Amsterdam. The architects responsible were **Hans van Heeswijk** and **Merkx + Girod**.

Though the building's exterior appears much as it did in 1683, the interior is filled with light and made more spacious by the removal of walls to create two large galleries. The former Church Hall is now used for receptions.

Exhibits and Facilities

The two **permanent exhibition** rooms in the Amstel Wing explore the relationship between the Netherlands and Russia—of which the Hermitage Amsterdam is a testament—and the history of patient care in Amsterdam, with a focus on elderly care at the Amstelhof. Recent and upcoming **temporary exhibits** include Art of the Russian Orthodox Church and Flemish Painters from the St. Petersburg Hermitage. The museum restaurant, Café Restaurant Neva, offers snacks and simple meals in addition to more lavish courses, inspired by the exhibits on view. The large **museum shop** stocks art, music and books on art as well as Russian literature. There is a children's museum shop in the Neerlandia building.

Allard Pierson Museum★

Oude Turfmarkt 127. Open Tue–Fri 10am–5pm, Sat–Sun and public holidays 1pm–5pm. Closed 1 Jan, Easter, 30 Apr, Whitsun, 25 Dec. €6.50, children 4-16 €3.25, under 4 free. 020 525 2556. www. allardpiersonmuseum.nl.

For a dose of the more remote past, this archaeological museum, part of Amsterdam University, has a remarkable collection of **antiquities**. It bears the name of an eminent professor of history of fine arts and letters at the unversity (1831-96). The building, in the neo-Classical style, was once the Nederlandsche Bank.

The first floor contains items from Egypt (such as **funerary masks★**, sculptures and Coptic textiles), the Middle East (Iranian pottery and jewelry), Syria, Anatolia, Palestine and Mesopotamia (including cylinder-seals and cuneiform writings). The second floor is devoted to Greece, Etruria and the Roman empire. The collection includes the **Amsterdam kouros★** (c. 590 BC), ceramics (including **red-figure jars★**), a Roman sarcophagus (c. AD 300) and various items of Etruscan earthenware and sculpture.

Cobra Museum voor Moderne Kunst★

Sandbergplein 1, Amstelveen. Open Tue–Sun 11am–5pm. Closed 1 Jan, 30 Apr and 25 Dec. €9.50, children 6-18 €5, under 6 free. 020 547 5050. www.cobra-museum.nl. Direct bus and tram connections to the museum's Amstelveen location, approximately 45min south of Amsterdam Centraal Station.

Amstelveen is a modern commuter town that has been the home of the Cobra Museum since 1995. The museum actively fosters the contemporary art scene in the town and in the Netherlands as a whole, with initiatives such as the Cobra Art Prize, which promotes Netherlands-based artists. First and foremost, the museum is dedicated to the short-lived but seminal **CoBrA movement**, with an emphasis on Cobra

Cobra Museum voor Moderne Kunst

MUST SEE

artists from the Low Countries, such as the Dutch artists **Karel Appel, Corneille** (Cornelis van Beverloo) and **Constant** (Constant Anton Nieuwenhuys) three of the movement's co-founders. The museum also takes into account, however, the influences, contemporary movements and artists and disciples of Cobra, all of which are bound to appear in the unique exhibits the museum stages several times a year. The museum does not exhibit its collection permanently, rather pieces are shown in rotation. The surprisingly light-filled building was designed by **Wim Quist**.

The Movement

In late 1948, six artists at a Paris cafe launched a movement that, while it lasted merely three years, caused a stir in the art world; its effects continue to be felt today. The name of this international movement derives from **C**openhagen, **B**russels, **A**msterdam. The Cobra movement emphasized freedom of color and form, a return to bolder, more "primitive" forms; its art revolutionized abstract expressionism in Europe, in addition to other movements and individual artists, some of whom remain active today.

Bijbels Museum

Herengracht 366. Open Mon–Sat 10am–5pm, Sun and holidays 11pm–5pm. Closed 1 Jan, 30 Apr, 25 and 26 Dec. €8, children 6-18 €4, under 6 free. 020 624 2436. www.bijbelsmuseum.nl.

Housed in a 17C canal house, the Bijbels Museum, or Bible Museum,

leaves no stone unturned. Its exhibits consider the history of the Bible from antiquity to its role in the Netherlands in the second millennium.

The biblical world is reconstructed with models like that of the Tabernacle, while authentic finds from biblical lands offer visitors a window into the ancient civilizations mentioned in the Scriptures. Dutch editions of the Bible are another major theme of the museum's collection, which includes the oldest Dutch Bible, printed in 1477, and centuries of its successors.

Het Grachtenhuis

Herengracht 386. Open Tue–Sun 10am–5pm. €8, children 6-18 €4, under 6 free. www.hetgrachtenhuis.nl.

The name Het Grachtenhuis, or The Canal House, is a reference to both the location and subject of this museum.

Situated on one of Amsterdam's most illustrious canals, the Grachtenhuis boasts an unusually wide façade bedecked with Classical ornamentation like a pediment and pilasters; it serves as a quintessential example of a posh 17C canal house.

Inside, however, the former residence now houses a public museum dedicated to Amsterdam's UNESCO World Heritage-enshrined **Canal Belt,** and the role it assumed during four centuries of the city's history. Spectacular multimedia displays are the cornerstone of the exhibits, which retell the history of the canals by means of maps, scale models, movies and more.

PARKS AND GARDENS

For a city that is so compact and built up, Amsterdam is surprisingly green, with more than 30 spacious verdant areas in or near the city where plant and bird life thrive. Vondelpark, south of city center, is the most popular urban park, but Amsterdamse Bos, farther south and near the airport, is a vast open greensward threaded by lakes and canals offering plenty of recreation. Not far from Artis, the formal grounds of Hortus Botanicus attract garden lovers of all ages, while in De Pijp, Sarphatipark, a small, beloved park, is ideal for picnics. Oosterpark and Westerpark have some of the city's loveliest shady waterfront lawns. All of these outdoor havens provide respite, beauty and exercise for residents and visitors alike.

URBAN GREENS

Vondelpark★★

Map inside front cover. Open 24hrs.

This 48ha/120 acre public park is located in the city center, west of Leidseplein and Museumplein and just outside of the canal ring. Walkers, cyclists, horseback-riders and inline skaters frequent the park as well as families, senior citizens, and young people out for a stroll. Mild weather and sunshine draw large numbers of people to the park's lawns and pond banks. Originally laid out in 1864 by D.J. Zocher, the park was extended in 1874 by his son, L.P. Zocher, in the style of English gardens. The park was the second stage of the project to create a greenbelt around the city center. First known as Nieuwe Park, it was named after the famous 17C Dutch poet and dramatist **Joost van den Vondel** when a statue in his honor was erected here in 1867.

Vondelpark covers a distance of almost 1.5km/1mi. It boasts a fine collection of more than 120 kinds of trees, including sweet chestnuts, oaks, poplars, swamp cypresses and catalpas. The park also has several wooded and paved trails, vast lawns, children's playgrounds, a rose garden and sparkling lakes, canals, ponds and fountains. In summer, free concerts are given in the open-air theater (**openluchttheater**).

EYE Film Institute

Vondelpark 3. Library open Mon–Tue & Thu–Fri; film show times vary. 020 589 1400. www.eyefilm.nl.
The former Filmmuseum has been subsumed under the EYE Film Institute, an umbrella organization

©Mats Stafseng Einarsen/Michelin

Vondelpark

comprising a number of cinema-related initiatives. Not quite a museum anymore, the building is open for visitors to browse its vast film library and attend monthly screenings and other events. Its exhaustive collection traces cinematic history from silent film to the present, and encompasses film-historical materials such as photos (especially stills), promotional posters, music, and film equipment in addition to the films themselves.

EYE is widely acclaimed for its masterful restoration of threatened films. Now in its final months in Vondelpark, EYE is slated to move to a dramatic new space on the northern bank of the IJ River in mid-2012.

Near the Park

♦ **Concertgebouw**
Concertgebouwplein 2-6. The famous concert hall (1888) is the home of the Royal Concertgebouw Orchestra; the title "Royal" was bestowed by Queen Beatrix to mark the orchestra's centenary. *See Performing Arts.*

♦ **Hollandsche Manege**
Vondelstraat 140, 020 618 0942, www.dehollandschemanege.nl. Call ahead since opening times vary. This riding school with an indoor ring dates from 1882. **A.L. van Gendt**, the architect, was clearly influenced by the Spanish Riding School in Vienna. Although the building was designed by Gendt, it was magnificently restored in 1986 under the direction of Prince Bernhardt. Still in use today, the Neoclassical building is decorated with stucco and cast iron. Riding lessons are available *(in Dutch*

Touring Tip

Several cafes can be found in and around the park, including the local favorite **'t Blauwe Theehuis**, or Blue Teahouse (*Vondelpark 5, 020 662 0254, www.blauwetheehuis.nl*); **Groot Melkhuis**, or Big Milkhouse (*Vondelpark 2, 020 612 9674, www.grootmelkhuis.nl*) with its popular children's playground; **Vondeltuin** (*Vondelpark 7, 062 756 5576, www.vondeltuin.nl*) with beach chairs and an outdoor cocktail bar; and **Café Vertigo** (*Vondelpark 3, 020 612 3021, www.vertigo.nl*) with a large, shady terrace.

only), but riders must bring their own riding boots.

Hortus Botanicus★

Map inside front cover. Plantage Middenlaan 2A. Open Mon–Fri 9am–5pm, Sat–Sun and public holidays 10am–5pm (Jul–Aug til 7pm). Closed 1 Jan, 12 Sept and 25 Dec. €7.50, children 5-14 €3.50. 020 625 9021. http://dehortus.nl.

At the request of the town's pharmacists and doctors, the University of Amsterdam laid out its botanical garden in1682 to grow medicinal plants that were, in many cases, supplied by the Dutch East India Company.

Today the garden houses more than 6,000 plants. In addition to the outdoor part of the garden, there is also a butterfly house, a large greenhouse representing three different climatic zones, and a palm house. The "House of Three Climates" has tropical plants,

PARKS AND GARDENS

including water lilies; the desert section features fauna from Africa and South America.Tradition has it that the first coffee plants grown outside Africa, producing Arabica, were germinated here.

Oosterpark

Map inside back cover. Linnaeus-straat, East Amsterdam. Open daily.

Located behind (south of) the Tropenmuseum *(see Districts)*, this large park encompasses grassy fields, waterfront lawns, a sculpture garden and a large, crescent-shaped pond that attracts a sizable bird population. Considered one of Amsterdam's most culturally diverse parks, Oosterpark was the first big public park to be created in the city by the Municipality of Amsterdam. It was designed by Leonard Anthony Springer, a Dutch landscape architect, in 1891. Popular with the local residents, the park is home to several events, including the Amsterdam Roots Festival *(see Calendar Of Events)*.

Sarphatipark

Map inside front cover. 1e Van der Helststraat, De Pijp. Open daily.

Located just south of the Albert Cuypmarkt in The Pijp neighborhood, Sarphatipark is a small, English-style park with a pond, an impressive fountain and wooden fencing. Laid out at the end of the 19C, the park pays homage to **Samuel Sarphati** (1813-66), who initiated many social projects in the district. It is the heart of De Pijp, Amsterdam's colorful "Latin Quarter" filled with people from all walks of life. In fact,

Sarphatipark is a good spot to people-watch. Its proximity to the Albert Cuypmarkt also makes it a popular setting for impromptu **picnics**.

Westerpark

Map inside back cover. North of Haarlemmerweg, West Amsterdam. Open daily.

Westerpark is one of the city's smaller public parks, but it offers open green space with a lake, paved paths and a canal-front lawn. The compact park entices passers-by to relax on the lawn, or take in a variety of contemporary public art, especially sculpture, on view.
The park was built in 1891 to serve as a local neighborhood park. Recently the surrounding area was renovated and extended. Westerpark is now part of the Culture Park **Westergasfabriek** (*Haarlemmerweg 8-10; 020 586 0710; www.westergasfabriek.nl/en*), a former gas factory with a cinema, restaurants and cafes. It is a venue for several of the city's events, concerts and festivals. The park surrounding Westergasfabriek includes a petting zoo, paddling pool, ponds and playgrounds.

OUTLYING PARKS

Amsterdamse Bos

Van Nijenrodeweg. Open daily. 020 644 5473. To book activities, go to www. amsterdamsebos.nl/algemene_ onderdelen/english_site.

Located south of Amsterdam, not far to the east of Schiphol airport, this immense park attracts

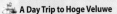

🚲 A Day Trip to Hoge Veluwe

The **Nationaal Park de Hoge Veluwe★★★** is located roughly 90km/56mi southeast of Amsterdam, near the city of Arnhem. Covering 5,500ha/13,585acres, this vast park is the nation's largest nature reserve. A unique combination of nature and culture, it contains the famous **Kröller-Müller Museum★★★**, the **St. Hubertus ★** hunting lodge, the **Museonder★** underground museum and countless sculptures and monuments. Worth a visit at any time of year, the park is served by **public transport** from Arnhem, Ede and Apeldoorn. Bus route 12 (from Arnhem) runs through the park from late March to late October. Allow half a day for your visit of the park, plus transportation to and from it.

The park's three **entrances** are located at Otterlo, Hoenderloo and Schaarsbergen. **Tickets** on sale at entrances provide entry to all sights except the Kröller-Müller Museum, which costs extra. At the Hoenderloo entrance, in the northeast, the **visitor center** (*open daily 9:30am–5pm, Apr–Oct til 6pm; 0900 464 3835; www.hogeveluwe.nl*) has a display on the history, flora and fauna of the park, as well as information on cycling, walking and wildlife viewing. **White bicycles** (*free of charge; available at park entrances, the visitor center and the Kröller-Müller Museum*) must be ridden on the paths and returned to the place of issue by end of the day. The park's desolate landscape of heathlands, grass, sand dunes and lakes is interspersed with stands of tall oak and beech trees, pine and birch woods. Rhododendrons flower in May and June, while August brings great expanses of purple heather. In autumn, the deciduous trees are brilliantly colored. Wildlife ranges from red deer, mouflons (wild sheep), wild boar and roe deer to a variety of birdlife. Mid-September to mid-October is the **rutting season** of the red deer. The best time to observe the animals is late afternoon when they are searching for food, in winter and spring (*until the end of May*). The park has **five game observatories**; the most accessible are De Klep and the Vogelvijvers (bird lakes).

many visitors to its wide range of facilities and amenities. Its name means Amsterdam Woods.

In October 1929, the Wall Street crash in the US caused a great depression in the 1930s. Unemployment in the Netherlands quadrupled in 1930, reaching 500,000 by 1935. To provide work for the unemployed—as many as 5,000 workers, Amsterdam's city council decided to lay out a vast area of polders as a landscaped park. The future park had to be totally drained before trees could be planted.

Some 300km/190mi of pipes were laid by the workforce, giving an idea of the scale of the project. Today the 800ha/1,977 acre park provides city dwellers and tourists an opportunity to escape the confines of urban life. There are 48km/30mi of cycling paths, 160km/100mi of footpaths, an open-air theater, a man-made hill for sledding in snowy winters, and several boating lakes.

The **Bosbaan**, a waterway that is more than 2km/1mi long, serves as an international rowing course.

JUST A JAUNT AWAY

Amsterdam has a convenient location within the Netherlands, not far from the coast, the southern banks of the IJsselmeer or the eastern interior. It is within an easy drive of several attractions that can be visited in a day or two. Holland's well known bulb fields at Keukenhof, the ceramics-rich city of Delft and the cheese market of Alkmaar are nearby sights not to be missed. Likewise, the windmills of Kinderdijk and traditional villages of Volendam and Marken have a special charm. So plan your transportation, reserve an overnight stay, and set out on a side trip filled with beauty and discovery.

SOUTH OF THE CITY

Haarlem★★

20km/12mi W of Amsterdam (30min drive).
From northwest Amsterdam, follow Haarlemmerweg (S103) west, which becomes N200, then A200.

Older than Amsterdam, the city of Haarlem was founded in the 10C. It is famous as the home of Dutch painter **Frans Hals** (c.1582-1666) and as the center of the large bulb-growing Keukenhof region. Just west of the Spaarne River, **Grote Markt★** square is flanked by a church, the town

hall, and former meat market. Several blocks south, in the heart of Old Haarlem, the **Frans Hals Museum★★★** *(Groot Heiligland 62; open Tue–Sat 11am–5pm, Sun noon–5pm; closed 25 Dec, 1 Jan; €10, children 18 and under free; www.franshalsmuseum.nl)* showcases the artist's famous civic guard and other portraits, marked by Hals' characteristic vitality and naturalness of style. (Of his 240 works, no fewer than 195 are portraits.) The **Teylers Museum★** *(Spaarne 16; 023 516 0960; www.teylersmuseum.nl)* includes exhibits of fossils, minerals, coins, and watercolors by Dutch masters. Due west of town, **Zandvoort★★★**

Bulb fields near Haarlem

©NBTC

Delftware

In the latter 17C, Delft acquired a reputation for making ceramics, a craft which soon spread over all of Europe. Heir to Italian majolica techniques, delftware is tin-glazed earthenware characterized by its remarkable lightness, and shine from a translucent coating. Traditional Dutch scenes included small boats sailing on canals spanned by humpback bridges. At first Delft was known for its monochrome painting of blues on a white background, still a characteristic today. Eventually production became more varied, and polychromy appeared. In the early 18C, delftware reached its peak. A decline set in rapidly, caused mainly by English competition and porcelain, made first in Germany. However, production continues today in several local factories.

is one of the busiest seaside resorts in the Netherlands. A large avenue runs along the dunes that overlook the beach. The famous Zandvoort **racing circuit** lies north of town, one of the sites of today's Formula 1 Grand Prix races.

Southeast of Haarlem, **Museum De Cruquius★** *(023 528 5704; www.museumdecruquius.nl)* is devoted to the fight against the sea and the creation of polders. An original **steam engine★** is on view.

🌷 Keukenhof★★

35km/22mi SW of Amsterdam (40min drive). From Amsterdam center, follow Nassaukade (S100) south and turn right onto Overtoom (S106); at the roundabout, take the second exit to continue on S106 (Surinameplein; becomes Cornelis Lelylaan). Merge left onto A10 toward The Hague. At Knooppunt De Nieuwe Meer, merge left onto A4/E19 toward The Hague. At exit 4 (Nieuw Vennep), merge onto N207 toward Lisse, then follow signs to Keukenhof. Public exhibit open late Mar–late May daily 8am–7:30pm. €14.50, children 4-11 €7. 025 246 5555. www.keukenhof.nl.

Since 1949 Keukenhof has served as the showplace for Dutch growers, drawing 900,000 annual visitors in recent years. Changing flower shows are held in the pavilions. The annual bulb market (Bloembollenmarkt) takes place in October.

In the 15C the site was Countess Jacoba van Beieren's kitchen garden (*keuken*: kitchen and *hof*: garden); she used the nearby castle as her hunting lodge. The castle grounds are landscaped in the English style with fountains, swan-filled lakes, themed gardens and works of art.

The brilliant colors of the tulips, hyacinths and narcissi are heightened by the cool greens of the grass and trees. **Orchids** are displayed in Koningin Beatrix Paviljoen. The **beeldenroute** is a trail that takes in some 50 art works. On the north side of the park, Keukenhof Windmill, built in the northern province of Groningen, offers a lovely **view** of the bulb fields.

Bulb Fields★★★

Bulbs have been grown in the region around Keukenhof for centuries. Today bulbs cover 14,400ha/35,583 acres across the

Netherlands. The main production areas are in the south of Haarlem and to the north of the line formed between Alkmaar and Hoorn. Three layers of bulbs are planted one on top of the other, providing new blooms throughout the season.

🏛 Delft★★

About 62km/39mi (1hr drive) SW of Amsterdam. From Amsterdam center, follow Nassaukade (S100) south and turn right onto Overtoom (S106); at the roundabout, take the second exit to continue on S106 (Surinameplein; turns into Cornelis Lelylaan). Merge left onto A10 toward The Hague. At Knooppunt De Nieuwe Meer, merge left onto A4/E19 toward The Hague. At the Knooppunt Ypenburg merge onto A13/E19 toward Delft; continue to exit 9 (Delft).

Delft is known the world over for its blue and white ceramics called **delftware**. With its tree-lined canals, Delft is one of the Netherlands' most charming

Kinderdijk Windmill

©NBTC

towns. It was home to artist **Johannes Vermeer** (1632-75) and naturalist **Antonie van Leeuwenhoek** (1632-1723). Once in Delft, head for the **Markt**: from there, whichever road you take will lead to the town's many treasures, including **Oude Kerk**, which holds Vermeer's tomb. Delft can be explored in a few hours, but an overnight stay will permit you to dine at a fine restaurant.

A few factories still make delftware by traditional methods. The following are open to the public:

- **Royal Delft**, Rotterdamseweg 196. *015 251 20 30. www.royaldelft.com.*
- **De Delftse Pauw**, Delftweg 133. *015 212 49 20. www.delftpottery.com.*
- **De Candelaer**, Kerkstraat 13. *015 213 18 48. www.candelaer.nl*

🏛 Kinderdijk Windmills★★

55km/34mi SW of Amsterdam (1.3hr drive). From Amsterdam center, head south to Stadhouderskade (S100) and turn left. Turn right onto Amsteldijk (S110), then left onto Nieuwe Utrechtseweg to continue on the S110, which becomes the A2. At Knooppunt Everdingen, merge onto A27/E311 toward Gorinchem; at Knooppunt Gorinchem, merge onto the A27/E311 toward Rotterdam. Take exit 22 (Alblasserdam) toward Kinderdijk; follow signs to Kinderdijk. Park open daily 24hrs. Museum windmill and pumping station open Apr–Oct daily 9:30am–5:30pm; Nov–Mar Sat–Sun 11am–4pm. www.kinderdijk.com.

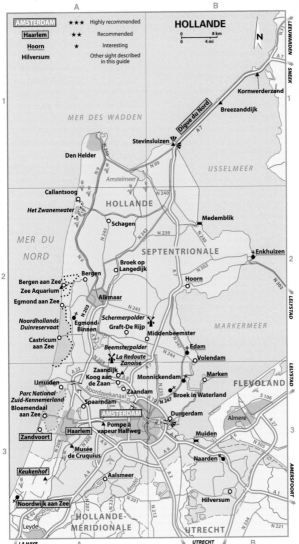

HOLLANDE

AMSTERDAM ★★★ Highly recommended
Haarlem ★★ Recommended
Hoorn ★ Interesting
Hilversum Other sight described in this guide

0   8 km
0   4 mi

N

LEEUWARDEN
SNEEK

Kornwerderzand
Breezanddijk

MER DES WADDEN

Digue du Nord

Stevinsluizen

Den Helder

IJSSELMEER

Amstelmeer

Callantsoog

HOLLANDE

Het Zwanenwater

Schagen

Medemblik

MER DU NORD

SEPTENTRIONALE

Enkhuizen

Broek op Langedijk

Hoorn

LELYSTAD

Bergen

Bergen aan Zee
Zee Aquarium
Egmond aan Zee

Alkmaar

Noordhollands Duinreservaat

Schermerpolder
Graft-De Rijp

Middenbeemster

MARKERMEER

Egmond-Binnen

Castricum aan Zee

Beemsterpolder

Edam

La Redoute Zanoise

Volendam

Zaandijk
Koog aan de Zaan

Monnickendam

Marken

LELYSTAD

FLEVOLAND

IJmuiden

Noordzeekanaal

Zaandam

Broek in Waterland

Parc National Zuid-Kennemerland

Spaarndam

Durgerdam

Almere

Bloemendaal aan Zee

AMSTERDAM

Pompe à vapeur Halfweg

Muiden

A 27

AMERSFOORT

Zandvoort

Haarlem

Musée de Cruquius

Naarden

Keukenhof

Aalsmeer

Noordwijk aan Zee

Hilversum

Leyde

HOLLANDE-MÉRIDIONALE

UTRECHT

LA HAYE

UTRECHT

Of the 1,000 mills still standing in the Netherlands, you can see 19 of them here. At the end of the village of **Kinderdijk**, an opening between the houses on the right gives a pretty **view** of the windmills. They line the *boezems* or drainage pools for the polderland near the Nederwaard pumping station. Their exceptional number, size, and beauty along the marshy plain earned them UNESCO World Heritage status in 1997. Until 1950, they helped drain the Alblasserwaard, which is below sea level; today, their sails turn for tourists only on designated Windmill Days.

Walk along the dykes or take a **boat tour** (*operates Apr–1 Oct 10am–5pm; €4, children €3; 062 224 8427*). The eight windmills of the Nederwaard are round stone **polder mills** dating from 1738. The interior of the second mill can be visited. Farther on is a smaller hollow post mill called De Blokker or Blokweerse Wip. Along the other canal, eight thatched windmills, octagonal in shape and with rotating caps, date from 1740. Hidden behind them are two windmills built in 1761.

NORTH OF THE CITY

🏛 Alkmaar★

45km/28mi NW of Amsterdam (50min drive). Take the IJ tunnel, then continue on the S116; merge right onto A10 toward S117. At Knooppunt Coenplein, merge onto A8/A22 toward Purmerend; take exit Wormer for N8/N246 toward Alkmaar. Turn right onto N8/N246; take the exit Uitgeest and merge onto N203/N8 toward Alkmaar. Merge right onto A9 towards Alkmaar; take exit 12 (Ring Alkmaar), then follow N9 to city center.

This historic town is best known for its weekly cheese market. Inside its surrounding moat, formed partly by the Noordhollandsch Kanaal, the old town has more or less preserved its 17C plan and a number of original façades.

The former fortifications have been transformed into a garden.

Allow two or three days to explore Alkmaar, including an hour at the **Kaasmarkt**. The **Hollands Kaasmuseum** tells the story of cheese-making. Spend one evening in the town to appreciate its lively atmosphere and fine restaurants. A **canal tour** (*45min*) is a great way to see the surrounding countryside; boats leave regularly from Mient Quay, near the cheese market.

Kaasmarkt★★

Open Apr–Sept Fri 10am–12:30pm. 072 511 4284.

Known since the early 17C, this traditional market is held on the Waagplein every Friday in spring and summer. Early in the morning, trucks bring Edam and Gouda cheeses to the square, where they are carefully piled up. At 10am buyers start tasting the cheeses and haggling; they seal an agreement with the seller by slapping hands. Then **cheese porters** (*kaasdragers*), wearing the traditional white clothes and straw hats, take over. These porters belong to an ancient guild, divided into companies identified by a different color (green, blue, red, and yellow) and consisting of six porters and a weigher or stacker (*tasman*).

🏛 Marken★

25km/16mi NE of Amsterdam (30min drive). Take the IJ tunnel, then continue on S116 to Nieuwe Leeuwarderweg (N247). Bear right onto Bernhardlaan, then make another right to continue on Bernhardlaan. At the roundabout, take the second exit onto

Traditional Dress

The women wear a wide skirt and a black apron over a striped petticoat. The striped blouse, worn in summer, is covered with a corselet and a printed front. The headdress is a brightly colored lace and cotton skullcap, from which a fringe of starched hair sometimes sticks out like a peak. The men wear a short waistcoat, baggy trousers tightened at the knees, and black socks. The children wear a costume more rarely; boys and girls wear a skirt and bonnet, but the shapes and colors differ. The costume worn on feast days is more elaborate.

Waterlandse Zeedijk (N518); once in Marken, this road turns into Kruisbaakweg.

Separated from the continent in the 13C during the formation of the Zuiderzee, Marken was an island 2.5km/1.5mi from shore until 1957. Now connected to the mainland, it sits on the edge of the Gouwzee, a sort of inland sea. From the beginning, Marken, whose population is Protestant, has formed a close community. With its wooden houses and townspeople attired in traditional dress (in season), it has preserved an atmosphere of olden times. An hour should be plenty of time if you confine your visit to the village, which consists of two quarters: **Havenbuurt**, near the port and **Kerkbuurt**, around the church. Subject to regular flooding in the past, the houses were grouped on small mounds and built on piles. Most are painted dark green, with slightly corbelled side gables; some are tarred and have roof tiles. The **interiors**, painted and polished, are richly ornamented. The box beds have a drawer that was used as a cradle. Dating to the first decade of the 20C, the **village church** has attractive stained-glass windows; inside is a collection of old photographs of Marken.

🚢 Volendam★

29km/18mi NE of Amsterdam (30min drive). Take the IJ tunnel, then continue on S116 to Nieuwe Leeuwarderweg (N247). Turn right onto Zeddeweg (N517); at the roundabout, take the first exit onto Kathammerzeedijk, which becomes Julianaweg. At the next roundabout, take the first exit onto Zeestraat.

A well-known port of the old Zuiderzee, Volendam, like Marken, sits on a small land-locked sea, Gouwzee. Unlike the people of Marken, its townspeople, who are mostly Catholic, wear the traditional costume in summer. It's best to head for Zeestraat, one of the town's few main streets, and follow its path to the harbor. Allow about three hours to explore the city's fine museums and harborside.

Volendams Museum
Zeestraat 41. Open mid-Mar–Oct daily 10am–5pm. €3, children €1.75. 029 936 9258. www.volendamsmuseum.nl.
Located in a small shop, this museum exhibits the national dress and ornaments as well as various works of art relating to the artists' colony that developed here at the end of the 19C.

JUST A JAUNT AWAY

115

OUTDOOR ACTIVITIES

Lots of the outdoor activities in Amsterdam are based on the canals and rivers, like the IJ, or the lakes outside city center, such as the Ijsselmeer and the Markermeer. Many activities within the historical center take place in the city's sports complexes and parks.

ACTIVITY SPORTS

Sports are a big part of the Dutch lifestyle: in Amsterdam alone there are about 800 sporting clubs. Favorite sports include leisurely cycling and skating as well as activities on the water such as sailing, rowing and windsurfing.

Bird Watching

Bird watching is a very popular activity in the Netherlands. The lakes, coastal areas, dunes, open meadows and woodlands around Amsterdam are great for spotting birds. Here are a couple of places to likely sight them:

De Oostvaardersplassen (*Kitsweg 1, 0320 254 5850*) is a popular area about 15km/25mi northeast of Amsterdam, near the town of Lelystad. The 57sq km/22sq mi nature reserve harbors a rich bird population, including some very rare species, in its marshes and grasslands. The marshland is at its best in May and June when the oilseed rape fields are in flower. The **Nationaal Park de Hoge Veluwe★★★** (*Deventerstraat 19; 055 577 285; www.theveluwe.com*) lies near the town of Apeldoorn, some 97km/60mi east of Amsterdam. The country's largest nature reserve covers 5,500ha/13,583 acres. Not only are there woodlands, heathlands and lakes that attract birds, there are also man-made attractions and recreational facilities (*see Parks and Gardens*).

Cycling

Amsterdam's flat and clearly marked cycleways make it ideal for touring the city center by bicycle. But if you're eager to get out of the city, **Amsterdamse Bos** (*see Parks and Gardens*) has a 14km/9mi cycle route through woodlands; bicycle rental is available at the main entrance. *See also Ideas and Tours, Bike Trips.* The ANWB (The Royal Dutch Touring Club) publishes cycle maps and routes that cross the country; bookstores and tourist offices stock them.

Fishing

Anglers will need a fishing license (VISpas) in order to fish; licenses can be obtained from the **Amsterdam Angling Association (AHV)**, 020 626 4988. You can fish at the Bosbaan in **Amsterdamse Bos** (*see above*), where it is possible to pick up a fishing license at the visitor center. To find more fishing spots around Amsterdam, visit *www.visplanner.nl.*

Golf

There are a number of golf courses in and around Amsterdam, and many excellent courses are open to non-members. Professional courses have requirements, however, such as a handicap. Call ahead for information, greens fees and tee times.

+ **Amsterdamse Golf Club**
  Bauduinlaan 35; *020 497 7866; www.amsterdamsegolfclub.nl*

- **Amsterdam Old Course**
  Zwarte Laantje 4; *020 694 3650;*
  www.amsterdamoldcourse.nl
- **De Hoge Dijk (Olympus)**
  Abcouderstraatweg *46; 029 428*
  1241; www.dehogedijk.nl
- **Golfclub Sloten**
  Sloterweg 1045; *020 614 2402;*
  www.golfbaansloten.nl

Skating
Ice-Skating
In the winter months when the
temperatures drop low enough,
Amsterdam's canals and waterways
freeze over. If you plan to take to
the ice like the locals, you will need
to buy your own skates, as there
are few places that rent them.
Caution: the ice may be thin or
weak, especially under bridges.
Remember to stay with large
groups of people and never skate
alone. A safer alternative would
be to skate at one of the **outdoor
ice rinks** that open in December
at Rembrandtplein, Museumplein
and Leidseplein. **Jaap Eden
Ijsbanen** (*Radioweg 64; 0900 724
2287; www.jaapeden.nl*) is a large
indoor and outdoor ice rink in east
Amsterdam.

In-line Skating
With its long flat stretches, the city
of Amsterdam is quite popular as
a place for in-line skating. Its large
park, Vondelpark (*see Parks and
Gardens*), is a favorite skating spot;
for skate rentals in the park, go to
Vondeltuin (*Vondelpark 7; 062
157 5885; www.vondeltuin.nl/
skaten*), which is located at the
southern end of the park.

- **Friday Night Skate**
  (*www.fridaynightskate.com*)
  takes place every Friday

evening, a communal gathering
for a 9mi-15mi skate through
the city. Everyone is free to join,
providing they can keep up.
Participants meet at
Vondelpark's EYE Institute,
weather permitting.

Swimming

Public Pools
Amsterdam has a handful
of outdoor swimming pools
(*closed Sept–Apr*).

- **De Mirandabad**
  (*De Mirandalaan 9; 020 252 4444*)
  is a large complex with indoor
  and outdoor pools, a wave
  machine, slides, and a solarium.
  Time slots are reserved, so call
  before you go.
- **Flevoparkbad** (*Insulindeweg
  1002; 020 692 5030; www.flevo
  park.nl*) is quite a popular
  outdoor swimming pool in
  Flevopark, a wild open space in
  East Amsterdam.

Waterways
Swimming is not recommended in
Amsterdam's canals or rivers. Some
people do swim in the canals,
but the water doesn't yet meet
standards of the 2006 European
Bathing Water Directive.

Water Sports
With its rivers, canals, waterways
and lakes, the city and outlying
areas of Amsterdam provide ample
opportunities to enjoy several
water sports.

Canoeing
- **Kano Verhuur Amsterdamse
  Bos** (*020 645 7831; www.kano
  verhuur-adam.nl*) has canoe
  rentals; it is located on the

Canoeing in Amsterdamse Bos

©NBTC

🚣 **Grote Vijver lake** in Amsterdamse Bos (*see Parks and Gardens*).

- **Watersportcentrum Sloterplas** in Amsterdam (*Christoffel Plantijngracht 4, 020 617 5839*).
- **Surf School Paradiso** in the town of Lelystad, about 15km/25mi northeast of Amsterdam (*Uilenweg 803 2025 6893, www.surfschool paradiso.nl*).

SAIL Amsterdam

©ATCB-

🚣 Rowing

- **The Bosbaan** (*020 545 6100*), in Amsterdams Bos, is a man-made rowing course measuring 2,300m/2,515yds. It hosts many rowing competitions.

Sailing and 🏄 Windsurfing

The Ijsselmeer, Markermeer and the Westeinderplassen (West End Lakes) are just some of several lakes around Amsterdam that offer rewarding sailing and windsurfing opportunities. Here are some picks to get you started:

- **Sailing School Pyxis Mare** in the town of Lelystad (about 25mi northeast of Amsterdam) is a sailing school for beginners and advanced sailors on the Markermeer (*Oostvaardersdijk 59c; 032 041 5000, www.zeil schoolpm.nl*). Boat rentals are available.
- **Surf Center IJberg** (*Pampuslaan and Bert Haanstrakade, 061 305 6663, www.surfcenterijburg.nl*) in Amsterdam offers windsurfing lessons and equipment rental.

SPECTATOR SPORTS

Amsterdam's fans enjoy regularly scheduled sporting events that include Eredivisie League Football (the highest-ranked football league in the Netherlands), rowing championships and sailing regattas, as well as exciting TT and cycling races in the surrounding regions.

Cycling

Held in April the **Amstel Gold Race** is the Netherlands' most popular and important road bicycle race. The course changes locations often, but is generally set in the south of the country.

Football Mania

Football is the national sport of the Netherlands and the Royal Dutch Football Association (KNVB) is the country's largest sports federation, with more than one million members. With devoted fans dressed in orange to cheer them, the Dutch football team is one of the world's strongest teams. Currently ranked number 1 in FIFA's world rankings, the Dutch team has competed in many World Cups and made the finals in 1974, 1978 and 2010. The team won the European Championship in 1988.

◆ **Amstel Gold Race Foundation,** Julianaweg 15, Sint Geertruid, *043 408 4167, www.amstelgoldrace.nl.* Amsterdam's velodrome hosts cycling events; for more information check the website.

◆ **Velodrome Amsterdam,** Sloterweg 1045, *020 408 2133, www.velodrome.nl.*

Rowing

One of the most popular and prestigious rowing championships in the Netherlands is the annual **Head of the River Amstel**; the 8km/5mi race from Amsterdam to Ouderkerk aan de Amstel is held in March.

◆ **The Willem III Rowing Club,** Jan Vroegopsingel 8, *020 665 4230, www.headoftheriver.nl.*

Soccer

Known as football in Europe, soccer is the most popular sport in the Netherlands. The local Amsterdam team **Ajax** is one of the most successful clubs in the world. Games at Amsterdam ArenA attract thousands of local fans. Soccer season is August and May; tickets should be booked well in advance.

◆ **AFC Ajax,** Arena Boulevard 29, Amsterdam Zuidoost, *020 311 1444, www.ajax.nl.* Tours of Amsterdam ArenA allow you to take a look behind the scenes; no reservations are necessary.

World of Ajax Tours

◆ **Amsterdam ArenA**, Arena Boulevard 1, Amsterdam Zuidoost, *020 311 1336, www.amsterdamarena.nl.*

Motorsports

A motorsport racetrack, the **TT Circuit** in Assen hosts several events, including car, motorcycle and truck races. Its most popular events are the **Dutch TT**, a motorcycling event that is part of the **MotoGP World Championship** (*Jun*) and the **Superbike World Championship** (*Apr*). Events attract thousands of spectators, so booking tickets and accommodations early is a must.

◆ **TT Circuit Assen,** De Haar 9, Assen, *0592 380380, www.tt-assen.com.*

Sailing

SAIL Amsterdam

Every five years in August some of the most impressive tall ships sail into the IJ River. The fleet includes hundreds of replicas, heritage crafts, modern ships and naval vessels. SAIL is one of the world's biggest maritime events, attracting more than 1.5 million spectators. For more information, contact:

◆ **Stitching Sail Amsterdam,** Kattenburgerstraat 7, *020 681 1804, www.sail2010.nl.*

FOR KIDS

Surprisingly, perhaps, Amsterdam is very accommodating to children. Where there is a park, there's a playground too. Many restaurants have menus for their pint-size patrons, and several attractions are definitely kid-centric in their focus. Here are a few places to take children for fun—and a mini-education in the process.

Artis★★

Plantage Kerklaan 38-40.
Open summer daily 9am–6pm;
winter daily 9am–5pm. €18.95,
children €15.50. 0900 278 4796.
www.artis.nl.

Artis opened its marvelously ornate gates as mainland Europe's first zoo in 1838; its diverse flora and fauna continue to enthrall children and adults. More than 900 animal species (mammals, reptiles and amphibians, birds, fish and insects) inhabit the zoo's 14ha/35 acres, which include a dedicated **aquarium★** and insectarium. The latest arrival is an elephant calf, born in 2011.

Never one to rest on its laurels, Artis recently added **Lemur Land**, where lovable primates frolic. The aquarium's Neoclassical architecture, which has earned it national monument status, provides a dramatic backdrop for the marine life. The 628sq m/ 6,760sq ft 🔭 **planetarium** takes audiences from the depths of the ocean to outer space by using vivid projections. Art, architecture, and nature lovers will all find enjoyment at Amsterdam's multi-faceted urban zoo.

Het Scheepvaart-museum★★

Kattenburgerplein 1.
Open daily 9am–5pm. €15,
children €0.50. 020 523 2222.
www.hetscheepvaartmuseum.nl.

Little else is more fundamental to Dutch history than the sea, a force the Netherlands has reckoned with for centuries. This is precisely the theme of the Dutch Maritime Museum, which looks at the rise of the Netherlands as a naval power and other matters maritime in its exhibits and activities. Ship ornaments, **nautical instruments**, and intricate models provide a visual snapshot of Dutch vessels. The museum offers special exhibits and virtual "adventures at sea" tailored to under-14-year-olds. The museum also dedicates an exhibit to its immediate environment, the **Port of Amsterdam**, in which the story of the port's rise to prominence within the context of Dutch and local history is narrated.

Sea lion at Artis

©Ronald van Weeren/Artis

MUST DO

The life-size ships in the museum's collection—an exact replica of the *Amsterdam*, a Dutch East Indies vessel that set sail in 1749, and a restored steamship from 1900—will impress the entire family.

NEMO★

Oosterdok 2. Open Tue–Sun 10am–5pm. €12.50, children under 3 free. 020 531 3233. www.e-nemo.nl.

Housed in a massive, jade green-colored "ship hull" on the Oosterdok (Eastern Dock), Science Center NEMO allows children to "explore, experiment and experience" the world and the science behind it. Its five floors of interactive and multimedia exhibits plumb the mysteries of the human body and mind, machines and electricity, the elements and more. Children are encouraged to conduct science experiments, both conventional and unconventional, in NEMO's Wonder Lab. Scientifically curious adults, even without children, are invited to join the fun. The spectacular **roof terrace** boasts a water park (*open in summer*), an annotated panorama of Amsterdam's skyline, and the Café DECK5, where diners can take in 360° views of Amsterdam, its harbor and historic center. NEMO is a must for science-savvy families.

Kinderboerderij de Pijp

Lizzy Ansinghstraat 82. Open Mon–Fri 11am–5pm, Sat–Sun 1pm–5pm. 020 664 8303. www.kinderboerderijdepijp.nl.

Leave the urban bustle and take the kids to an oasis of **farmland** in Amsterdam's Old South. Since 1985 this children's farm has offered close encounters with farm animals and fowl, as well as nature-oriented activities. Children are free to pet donkeys, sheep, ponies and other creatures that roam the farm. Supervised cuddle sessions introduce children to more timid animals like rabbits and chicks; others, like radiant peacocks and talkative hens, can be admired from afar. Workshops teach children about animal life and nature's products that meet our daily needs, from wool and other fibers, to paper and even apple pie.

TunFun Speelpark

Mr. Visserplein 7. Open daily 10am–6pm. 18 and older free, children 1-12 €7.50. 020 689 4300. www.tunfun.nl.

In most cities a forsaken traffic underpass would become an eyesore; in Amsterdam—a pioneer of sustainable urban solutions—it became a well-loved children's park. Billed as a place where kids from 1 to 12 can "play outside indoors," the 4,000sq m/4,784sq yd space provides room for active fun, with slides, ball pits, **trampolines,** inflatable bounce houses, soccer fields and dance floors. At the HapSap cafe, adults can relax with an espresso, or surf the web on TunFun's Wi-Fi connection. Under their community-oriented philosophy, TunFun supports charities for children who are disabled, ill or in need with donation drives and other initiatives, so that part of the admission fee is ultimately siphoned back into the community.

PERFORMING ARTS

Amsterdam's lively cultural scene is disproportionately large compared to the city's size. Lots of big names in the classical music world come here as part of their international touring circuit. English-language theater is more limited, but possible to find. Dance, especially classical ballet and contemporary, is easy to come by. Real culture vultures should not miss two events: the Holland Festival, an annual celebration of performing arts held in venues throughout the city in June, and the Grachtenfestival featuring classical music performances staged on Amsterdam's historic canal belt every August.

Classical Music and Opera

Beurs van Berlage★
*Damrak 243. 020 530 4141.
www.beursvanberlage.nl.*
Housed in architect H.P. Berlage's former Stock Exchange (*see Architecture*), the 1903 Beurs van Berlage is an atmospheric venue steeped in history.
Events take place here throughout the year. The concert hall occupies what was once the stock exchange itself, and a rehearsal room sits in the former grain exchange.
The space has been used by the **Netherlands Philharmonic Orchestra** and the **Netherlands Chamber Orchestra** as well as other classical musicians.
Find out what's on before you go, however, because the building is used for corporate events, too.

Het Bimhuis
*Piet Heinkade 3. 020 788 2150.
www.bimhuis.nl*
The black box protruding from the side of the Muziekgebouw is a world-class performance space for jazz and improvisational music. A venue with a view, the Bimhuis overlooks the IJ River—the stretch of water behind Centraal Station that separates Amsterdam North

from the center of town. Opened in 2003 the Bimhuis stages mainly jazz performances, with classic international names in the genre such as the Jon Irabagon Trio and the Orchestre National de Jazz. Performances number as many as 300 a year, and have featured the likes of Charles Mingus, Archie Shepp, Cecil Taylor, Pharoah Sanders and Sun Ra.

Concertgebouw
Concertgebouwplein 10. 0900 671 8345. www.concertgebouw.nl.
Home to the world-famous **Royal Concertgebouw Orchestra**, the Concertgebouw, built in 1888, is the country's top concert hall, known for its excellent acoustics. The title "Royal" was bestowed by Queen Beatrix to mark the orchestra's centenary.

The premier venue specializes in orchestral music that is presented in either of its two auditoriums. Located just south of Amsterdam's museum square, the concert hall is popular with visitors and residents alike for its classical concerts from Bach and Brahms to opera and piano solos.

Felix Meritis
Keizersgracht 324. 020 623 1311. www.felixmeritis.nl.
Calling itself the European Centre for Arts, Culture and Science, Felix Meritis offers a variety of high-brow entertainment. Recent cultural events have included performances by classical musicians Ensemble Caméléon and pianist Igor Roma, as well as a re-interpretation of Shakespeare's *Hamlet*.

Koninklijk Theater Carré
Amstel 115-125. 0900 252 5255. www.theatercarre.nl.
Housed in an enormous (and very grand) building overlooking the Amstel River, the Carré started as a circus venue in the 19C. Since then, it has gone on to offer musicals, dance shows, opera, stand-up comedy and music concerts, with performances suitable for both adults and children.

Muziekgebouw aan het IJ
Piet Heinkade 1. 020 788 2010. www.muziekgebouw.nl
This modern building overlooking the IJ was designed by Danish architectural firm 3XN; its remarkable form has been described by a Dutch newspaper as "a box within a box within a box." Classical music dominates the concert calendar, but jazz, electronic and non-Western music are performed too.

Muziektheater (Stopera)
Waterlooplein 22. 020 551 8117. www.muziektheater.nl.
The 1987 Stopera (from *stadhuis* and *opera*) is known particularly for its opera and dance. Big names in the Netherlands, such as the Nederlandse Opera, Nationale Ballet, Nederlands Dans Theater, and Holland Symfonia have all performed here. The Nederlandse Opera's repertoire includes classic operas such as *Romeo and Juliet, Elektra* and *Don Carlo. Dionysos* premiered in 2010. Shows in the 1,689-seat theater are not inexpensive, but they are generally worth the price of the ticket.

Stadsschouwburg
Leidseplein 26. 020 624 2311. www.stadsschouwburg amsterdam.nl.
Built in 1894 this theater has recently acquired a fashionable new bar and restaurant (named the Stanislavski) that attract an altogether hipper crowd. The theater's two concert halls—seating audiences of 900 and 520 respectively—showcase a variety of music, dance and theater. The **Toneelgroep Amsterdam** *(see below)* calls the theater home.

🎭 Openluchttheater
Vondelpark 0. Open Jun–Aug
Fri & Sun. 020 673 1499.
www.openluchttheater.nl.
Open Friday through Sunday in
summer, this open-air theater sits
right in the middle of the city's
most popular park: the Vondelpark
(*see Parks and Gardens*). Classical
music fans should head to the
park on Sunday at lunchtime,
since the Nederlands Philharmonic
Orchestra and Dutch National
Opera Academy have both
performed here. Friday evenings
are reserved for modern dance,
with recent performances by
Dansgroep Amsterdam and
Scapino Ballet Rotterdam.

Theater
Betty Asfalt Complex
Nieuwezijds Voorburgwal 280-2.
020 620 4748. www.bettyasfalt.nl
Known for profiling up-and-
coming artists, this complex
attracts an alternative crowd. One
recently acclaimed performance
put on here was the Edinburgh
Fringe Festival hit, *You're Not Like
the Other Girls, Chrissy*.

Crea
*Turfdraagsterpad 17. 020 525
1400. www.crea.uva.nl.*
Located next to the University
of Amsterdam, the Crea offers
student-friendly culture at student-
friendly prices. As well as weekly
comedy nights hosting improvised
and amateur stand-up comedy,
you can expect the latest in dance
choreography, amateur orchestras
and docu-film screenings.

De Kleine Komedie
Amstel 56- 58. 020 626 5917.
www.dekleinekomedie.nl.
Despite its name, De Kleine
Komedie is about more than just
comedy. Situated on the Amstel
river, the theater showcases
cabaret, music performances,
and cross-genre shows such as
"flamenco opera."

DeLaMar Theater
Marnixstraat 402. 020 555 26 27.
www.delamar.nl.
A brand new theater right by the
Leidseplein, DeLaMar is already
attracting big-name productions
in plays, music and dance.
The agenda so far has included
Stomp, The Magic Flute, and a
dance ode to Stravinski.

DeLaMar Theater

©Jan Theun van Rees/DeLaMar Theater

🎭 Melkweg
Lijnbaansgracht 234. 020 531 8181.
www.melkweg.nl.
While the Melkweg is better
known for its music scene, its
theater also hosts regular dance
performances by both Dutch and
international troupes. You can
expect contemporary rather than
classical choreographies.

Art-House Cinema

Amsterdam is one of only a handful of European cities that still has plenty of independent art-house cinemas, most of which have been in operation for decades. But think twice before you book tickets to watch a European film, because the subtitles may be in Dutch. Art-house movies, indie flicks, low-budget English-language and foreign films are all offered at Amsterdam's old-fashioned movie theaters, including **The Movies** *(Haarlemmerdijk 161-3; 020 626 7069; www.themovies.nl)*, **Cinecenter** *(Lijnbaansgracht 236; 020 623 6615; www.cinecenter.nl)*, the **Kriterion** *(Roetersstraat 170; 020 623 1708; www.kriterion.nl)* **Uitkijk** *(Prinsengracht 452; 020 623 7460; www.uitkijk.nl)* and **Rialto** *(Ceintuurbaan 338; 020 662 3488; www.rialtofilm.nl)*.

Theater Fabriek Amsterdam
Czaar Peterstraat 213. 020 522 5260. www.theaterfabriek amsterdam.nl.

Out of city center in Amsterdam East, this theater offers music concerts, cabaret and other performances, with a bent toward family shows that are suitable for children. *The Best of Sesame Street* was recently running at this new theater that seats more than a thousand people.

Performing Arts Groups

Het Nationale Ballet
Waterlooplein 22. 020 551 8225. www.het-nationale-ballet.nl.

The Netherlands' national ballet troupe is definitely of international quality. *Don Quixote, Sleeping Beauty, Giselle* and other classics have all been performed by the flawless dancers, usually at the Muziektheater.

Toneelgroep Amsterdam
Marnixstraat 427. 020 795 9900. www.toneelgroepamsterdam.nl.

The largest association of actors in the Netherlands, the Toneelgroep performs at the Stadsschouwburg on the Leidseplein. Led by director Ivo van Hove, a core group of the top 21 actors performs plays with international appeal, including *Angels in America* and *Macbeth*.

Performance of Antonioni Project, Toneelgroep Amsterdam

© Jan Versweyveld/Toneelgroep Amsterdam

PERFORMING ARTS

SHOPPING

A dynamic and inventive city, Amsterdam offers a rewarding shopping experience for visitors seeking avant-garde creations as well as traditional wares. The city is home to luxurious department stores housed in historic buildings, chic boutiques tucked away in narrow streets, unusual specialty shops, colorful outdoor markets with artisanal food stalls. So plan your strategy and begin your shopping.

Before You Buy

Opening Hours – Normal shopping hours are 9am–6pm Mon–Wed and Fri. Many shops outside the main tourist areas are closed Mon. Shops in the city center are closed Mon mornings. On Thursdays most shops stay open until 9pm. On weekends, shops close at 5pm.

Sales Tax – In shops, the **Value Added Tax** (VAT) is included in the price tag (see Basic Information). Upon leaving the EU within three months of purchase, non-European Union residents are entitled to a VAT refund of up to 18 percent on single purchases of more than €50. For more information, or to register for a refund online, visit *www.vatfree.nl*.

Amsterdam Specialties

Popular Dutch souvenirs are decorative and wearable **clogs** (*klompen*), small painted windmills, canal houses and costume dolls. Tulip and other **flower bulbs** are also favorite purchases. More serious acquisitions are **Delft pottery** (*www.royaldelft.com*) and **diamonds**, for which the city is well known; a number of local sellers and factories also offer tours (see below). When it comes to **cheese**, Amsterdam has an excellent selection of both local and regional varieties. Most cheese shops will allow customers to sample their merchandise before purchase. Note that Gouda is not a protected name, so it can be manufactured anywhere; most Gouda cheeses are not made by individual farms, but are produced on an industrial scale.

Department Stores and Shopping Centers

◆ **De Bijenkorf** (*Dam 1, 0900 09 19, www.bijenkorf.nl*) is a luxurious department store offering top brands and regular sales; it is popular with local residents.
◆ **Magna Plaza** (*Nieuwezijds Voorburgwal 182, 020 626 9199, www.magnaplaza.nl*) is an upscale indoor shopping center with some 40 stores.

Cheese

©ATCB

MUST DO

◆ **Maison de Bonneterie**
(*Rokin 140-142, 020 531 4300,*
www.debonneterie.nl) is a high-end
department store specializing in
fashions from some of the world's
leading designers. It is housed in a
magnificent historical building.
◆ **Metz & Co.** (*Leidsestraat 34-36,*
020 520 7020, www.metzco.eu) is
an exclusive luxury department
store that stocks goods from
glassware to clothing. On the top
floor is a popular cafe.
◆ **Vroom & Dreesman**
(*Kalverstraat 203, 0900 235 8363,*
www.vd.nl) is the Netherlands'
largest department store chain.
Usually referred to as V&D by
the Dutch, the stores sell good
quality yet affordable clothing,
housewares and cosmetics.

Fashion

There are plenty of exclusive
and trendy fashion stores, shoe
shops and jewelers to be found
along Amsterdam's shopping
streets. Shoppers seeking haute
couture fashion should check out
Amsterdam's department stores
on **Dam square**, as well as in the
Museum Quarter, particularly
along the streets **P.C. Hooftstraat**
and **Van Baerlesstraat**. The
pedestrianized and lively streets
Kalverstraat and **Nieuwendijk**
are Amsterdam's most popular
shopping areas; they house many
more down-to-earth clothing
shops as well as shoe shops. The **9
Streets** (*see sidebar*), the Jordaan
district, Haarlemmerstraat and
Utrechtstraat are the places to go
for boutiques and specialty fashion
shops.
◆ **Marlies Dekkers**
(*Berenstraat 18, 020 421 1900 and*
Cornelis Schuytstraat 13, 020 471

The 9 Streets
De 9 Straatjes are a
boutique lover's paradise
set in the charming streets
between the Leidsestraat and
the Raadhuisstraat within
Amsterdam's historic canal ring.
Here you'll find a mix of fashion
boutiques, vintage shops,
specialized stores for books and
music, art galleries and gourmet
shops. Restaurants and cafes
abound in which to take a break
and enjoy the atmosphere of this
local hot spot.

4146, www.marliesdekkers.com)
is the outlet for luxurious, trend-
setting lingerie made by renowned
Dutch fashion designer Marlies
Dekkers.
◆ **De Maagd & De Leeuw**
(*Hartenstraat 32, 020 428 0047,*
www.demaagdendeleeuw.nl) is the
place to find the latest trends from
Paris; the small boutique updates
its inventory every 4 to 6 weeks.
◆ **Cherry Sue**
(*Eerste Leliedwarsstraat 6, 020*
623 3766, www.cherrysue.com)
appeals to vintage fashion lovers
who appreciate 1950s inspired
designs; if you wish, dresses can
also be custom-made using your
own fabric.

Diamond Factories

About 10 of the city's
manufacturers are open to
the public; a handful of them
offer tours. Here are two:
◆ **Gassan Diamonds** (*Nieuwe*
Uilenburgerstraat 173-175, 020 622
5333, www.gassandiamonds.com)
is open Mon–Sun 9am–5pm.
◆ **Coster Diamonds** (*Paulus*
Potterstraat 2-6, 020 305 5555,

www.costerdiamonds.com) is open Mon–Sun 9am–5pm.

Markets

◆ **Albert Cuypmarkt★** *(Albert Cuypstraat, Mon–Sat 9am–5pm)* is the city's most popular local market, selling general goods with bargains on food, clothes, housewares and fabric. Very large in size, the market comprises some 300 stalls plus 100 or so shops.

◆ **Flower Market★★** *(Singel, between Muntplein and Koningsplein, Mon–Sat 9am–5:30pm, Sun 11am–5:30pm)* is a colorful market with fresh flowers, plants, bulbs, souvenirs and gifts.

◆ **Organic Farmers' Market** *(Noodermarkt on the Prinsengracht, Sat 9am–5pm)* offers artisanal cheeses, honey, baked goods and more. A flea market also sets up nearby. The Noordermarkt is the site of a weekly **Boerenmarkt** *(Sat 9am–6pm; www.boerenmarkt amsterdam.nl)*, the country's first farmers' market and now an Amsterdam institution.

◆ **Waterlooplein Flea Market** *(Waterlooplein, Mon–Sat 9am–5pm)* is full of bric-a-brac, antiques, used goods and contemporary wares.

◆ **Spui Book Market** *(Spui, Fri 10am–6pm)* carries antique and used books, maps and prints.

◆ **Spui Art Market** *(Spui, Mar–Dec, Sun 10am–6pm)* showcases local and regional artists selling original prints, oil paintings, watercolors, sculpture, jewelry, ceramics and more.

Art and Antiques

Most of Amsterdam's antique shops are located on the streets **Spiegelstraat, Nieuwe Spiegelstraat** and **Kerkstraat**; others dot the main canal area around the Singel, Herengracht, Keizersgracht and Prinsengracht.

◆ **Antiekcentrum Amsterdam** *(Elandsgracht 109, 020 624 9038, www.antiekcentrumamsterdam.com)* is a 1,750sq m/2,093sq yd antique center that offers a vast assortment of antiques, art and collectibles as well as a market on Wed, Sat and Sun.

◆ **Droomfabriek** *(Nieuwe Spiegelstraat 9B, 020 620 0760, www.droomfabriekantiek.nl)* holds a glamorous collection of vintage costume jewelry and handbags from leading fashion designers.

◆ **The Rock Archive** *(Prinsengracht 110BG, 020 423 0489, www.rock archive.nl)* is a repository of fine art photography of rock and jazz icons shot by the world's best music photographers.

◆ **Van Hier Tot Tokio** *(Prinsengracht 262, 020 428 2682 and Rozengracht 184, 020 423 4599, www.vanhiertottokio.com)*

Antiques Quarter
Art and antiques enthusiasts should visit Amsterdam's art and antique district known as the **Spiegelkwartier**, located mainly on Spiegelstraat and Nieuwe Spiegelstraat. This picturesque hub is occupied by more than 70 specialized stores selling contemporary and traditional art, Art Deco jewelry, Chinese artifacts, Delftware, antique maps and much more. Recently the district has been experiencing a revival with an infusion of new fashion and specialty food shops, and cafes and restaurants in among the older galleries and antique stores.

Authentic Japanese textiles, art and furniture for sale at two locations.

Souvenirs

◆ **De Bollemand - The Bulb Basket** *(Prinsengracht 116, 020 421 0095, www.amsterdam tulipmuseum.nl)* stocks all things tulip: bulbs, books, stationery, tiles, home decor and more.

◆ De Klompenboer - **Wooden Shoe Factory** *(Sint Antoniesbreestraat 39-51, 020 427 3862, www.woodenshoefactory.com)* carries traditional and modern clogs in all colors and sizes. Clogs also come hand-painted or can be custom-ordered.

◆ **Galleria D'Arte Rinascimento** *(Prinsengracht 170, 020 622 7509, www.delft-art-gallery.com)* is a small shop packed with an excellent collection of old and new Delft pottery.

Books

◆ **American Book Center** *(Spui 12, 020 625 5537, www.abc.nl)* houses a huge selection of English-language books and magazines.

◆ **Book Exchange** *(Kloveniersburgwal 58, 020 626 6266, www.bookexchange.nl)* sells second-hand English books.

Food

◆ **Puccini Bomboni** *(Singel 184, 020 427 8341 and Staalstraat 17, 020 626 5474, www.puccinibomboni.com)* makes fine chocolates by hand on the premises using a special recipe. Two locations.

◆ **Reypenaer** *(Singel 182, 020 320 6333, www.wijngaardkaas.nl)* is a shop and tasting room offering excellent artisanal Gouda, produced by a family business dating back more than 100 years.

On Wed–Sun the shop hosts cheese tasting for a small price.

Specialty Shops

◆ **De Sprookjeskamer - The Fairytale Shop** *(Nieuwezijds Voorburgwal 383, 020 420 0015, www.desprookjeskamer.nl)* is a small store packed with all things make believe—and red and white polka dot.

◆ **The Christmas Palace** *(Singel 508-510, 020 421 0155, www.christmas-palace.com)* is a cozy shop near the flower market that overflows with Christmas decorations and ornaments.

◆ **The Condomerie** *(Warmoesstraat 141, 020 627 4174, www.condomerie.com)* is a little store that prides itself on a large variety of condoms available in all shapes, sizes and colors.

◆ **Droog** *(Staalstraat 7B, 020 523 5059, www.droog.com)* presents Dutch designs in home accessories, lighting and furniture. The shop also houses art and design installations.

Delftware and other creations

©Mats Stafseng Einarsen/Michelin

NIGHTLIFE

Amsterdam has a lively night scene—everything from quiet, cozy bars to packed-out, late-night clubs. Apart from the red-light district, **Leidseplein**, **Rembrandtplein** and **Thorbeckeplein** are busy in the evening, with many night spots. Most nightclubs have DJs, acts and music styles on different nights, so it's a good idea to check what's on in advance. Local weekly and monthly publications such as *Uitkrant* and the English-language magazine *Time Out Amsterdam* list club nights, music concerts and other entertainment; they are available at most large news agents and many major hotels.

Bars

Cafe de Sluyswacht

Jodenbreestraat 1, Waterlooplein.
020 625 7611. www.sluyswacht.nl.
This cheerful little waterside cafe lies opposite the Rembrandthuis. The terrace offers a view of the Oudeschans. Don't worry if you've had a glass or two and things look a little strange; it's the building that's leaning at an angle, not you.

De Prins

Prinsengracht 124, Canals Area.
020 624 9382. www.deprins.nl.
Right near the Anne Frank Huis and overlooking one of Amsterdam's grandest canals, De Prins is a great place to people-watch while sipping an early evening beer on the sunny terrace.

Be sure to order a portion of *ossenworst* (raw, smoked beef sausage), an Amsterdam specialty, or *bitterballen* (deep-fried, breaded meat-filled balls) as a **snack** to go with your *biertje*.

Finch

Noordermarkt 5, Jordaan.
020 626 2461.
Sitting next door to Proust (*opposite*), Finch has recently been revamped with comfortable leather chairs, dark wall paint and a funky vintage feel to the design. The drinks may be the same, but wine now comes in proper wine

---

Best Views at Night

Some Amsterdam businesses are privy to their own picturesque views, especially at night. **Cafe Blue** (*Singel 457, 3rd floor; 020 427 3901; www.blue-amsterdam.nl*) trades solid walls for windows with 360° views on the top floor of the Kalvertoren, a multi-level matrix of retail chains off Kalverstraat. Cafe and restaurant chain **La Place** (*multiple locations; www.laplace.nl*) often boasts the best views in any Dutch town, including Amsterdam.
The multistorey **Vroom & Dreesman** department store (*Kalverstraat 203; www.vd.nl*) and **Openbaare Bibliotheek Amsterdam** (*Amsterdam Public Library, Oosterdokskade 143; www.oba.nl*) afford great views. For a more upscale experience, sample one of the city's best cocktails at **Twenty Third Bar** on the 23rd floor of the posh **Hotel Okura** (*Ferdinand Bolstraat 333; www.okura.nl*), or reserve a window-side table next door at **Ciel Bleu** (*www.cielbleu.nl*), whose menu offers caviar, oysters and truffle-laced dishes.

MUST DO

glasses, as opposed to the beakers in which it so frequently appears at other Amsterdam establishments.

Kamer 401
Marnixstraat 401, Canals Area.
020 620 0614. www.kamer401.nl.
One of three bars next door to each other on Marnixstraat, Kamer offers a cool, relaxed interior that is typical of this little nightlife enclave. Arrive early if you want a seat, as the venue fills up as soon as the concerts and gigs at the Melkweg next door are finished.

Morlang
Keizersgracht 451, Canals Area.
020 625 2681. www.morlang.nl.
Neighboring the Walem (*below*), Morlang attracts a similarly young and hip crowd. Its prime location close to the busy Leidsestraat shopping street makes it a popular place to hang out on the terrace in late afternoon.

Poco Loco
Nieuwmarkt 24, Oude Zijde.
020 624 2937. www.diningcity.nl/
pocoloco.
With a retro 1970s twist to its interior, Poco Loco welcomes you for morning coffee, an afternoon beer or a late-night cocktail. This hangout also serves tapas, which make a great way to soak up the alcohol at the same time. In winter, ask for a glass of hot, fragrant *gluhwein* (mulled wine).

Proust
Noordermarkt 4, Jordaan. 020
6239145. www.goodfoodgroup.nl.
With a giant lit-up gun made of glittering glass and metal hanging over the bar above the ceiling, Proust sets a dramatic tone to its

space. Farther back, however, the lighting is more subdued, making the perfect place for a cozy catch-up over beer or a glass of wine.

VOC
Prins Hendrikkade 94-95,
Port Area. 020 428 8291.
www.schreierstoren.nl.
VOC stands for Vereenigde Oostindische Compagnie (United East Indies Company). Recalling Amsterdam's sea-faring heyday, this nautically themed cafe has two rooms, one furnished with antiques and the other used as a reading room. It also has two terraces, one beside the IJ waterfront, on which to enjoy a drink and a sunny day.

Walem
Keizersgracht 449, Canals Area.
020 625 3544. www.walem.nl.
The place to see and be seen, Walem harbors a designer interior that matches its creative clientele. The bar has a leafy garden at the rear of the property, which is a great spot for an afternoon glass of cool wine during the warm days of summer.

Walem and Morlang

©Greg Gladman/Apa Publications

NIGHTLIFE

Werck

Prinsengracht 277, Canals Area.
020 627 4079. www.werck.nl.
A former coachhouse once
belonging to Westerkerk (West
Church) next door, this big, breezy
venue is atypical of Amsterdam's
bar scene. As well as cocktails and
a decent wine list, Werck lays on
DJs Friday and Saturday nights so
patrons can dance until 3am.

Nightclubs

Escape

Rembrandtplein 11, Nieuwe Zijde.
020 622 1111. www.escape.nl.
Escape is Amsterdam's largest club,
right in the middle of Amsterdam's
biggest clubbing area, the
Rembrandtplein. It's an extravagant
venue with go-go girls, drag queens
and special gay evenings.

Hotel Arena

's-Gravesandestraat 51,
Plantage. 020 850 2400.
www.hotelarena.nl.
As well as being able to sleep, eat
and drink at this hotel, you can
party in its giant clubbing space.
With regular 1980s and 90s nights,
Latino parties and Asian beats,
the agenda holds something for
everyone.

Jimmy Woo

Korte Leidsedwarsstraat 18,
Canals Area. 020 626 3150.
www.jimmywoo.com.
Fashionistas and glamorous types
hang out here, and the decor
matches the clientele. Music on
club nights ranges from R and B
and 90s classics to techno and
everything in between. Be sure
to check out the program for
something that suits your tastes.

Odeon

©ATCB

Odeon

Singel 460, Canals Area. 020 521
8555. www.odeontheater.nl.
In the middle of the action,
between Leidseplein,
Rembrandtplein and Spui, the
Odeon sits on the picturesque
Singel canal. Club nights are held
in a concert room with a balcony
overlooking the dance floor. On
Friday and Saturday evenings,
Dutch and international DJs spin
old classics and new tunes.

Studio 80

Rembrandtplein 17, Nieuwe Zijde.
020 521 8333. www.studio80.nl.
One of the less commercial clubs
on Rembrandtplein, Studio 80
prides itself on being a platform for
new DJs and musical acts. Some
of its club nights have become
internationally famous, with party
goers coming from far and wide
for M.U.L.T.I.S.E.X.Y., where you can
expect an open-minded mix of
gay, straight and bisexual clubbers.

Sugar Factory

Lijnbaansgracht 238,
Canals Area. 020 627 0008.
www.sugarfactory.nl.
Calling itself a "night theater," Sugar
Factory is multi-disciplinary. Music
meets comedy meets performance
art, and more. Electro-music night

Electronation was recently held here, and Sugar Factory's central location just off Leidseplein attracts well-known international DJs like Giles Peterson.

Trouw
Wibautstraat 131,
East Amsterdam. 020 463 7788.
www.trouwamsterdam.nl.
Wibautstraat parallels the Amstel River west of Oosterpark. Housed in the converted buildings of one of the Netherlands' best known newspapers, Trouw is named after the publication that was once produced here. The club sits atop the building, with a great view of the city. It offers a variety of music with a preference for electro.

Winston
Warmoesstraat 123, Oude Zijde.
020 623 1380. www.winston.nl.
Located in the heart of the red-light district, this club has a grungy, underground feel to it, attracting an eclectic clientele. Open seven nights a week until the early hours, Winston offers a music spectrum that includes indie-rock, electro, drum 'n bass, hip hop, dub-reggae, retro-pop and disco. Most nights involve some kind of live act earlier in the evening.

Live Entertainment

Amsterdam ArenA
Arena Boulevard 1, Bijlmermeer.
020 311 1333. www.amsterdam
arena.nl.
Located in the southeast suburb of Bijlmermeer, this giant arena is home to Ajax, Amsterdam's football club. It is used for large concerts when it's not being used by the football team. Huge

international names like Take That have played here, which is no surprise given the venue's capacity for more than 50,000 people.

Amsterdam RAI Theater
Europaplein 22, South Amsterdam.
020 549 1212. www.rai.nl.
One of the largest theater venues in Amsterdam, the RAI Theater resides within the mammoth RAI Exhibition Center located on the south side of the city. It presents various Dutch and international productions. Recent performances have included a global- touring Bollywood dance show, as well as the famous Michael Jackson tribute, "Man in the Mirror."

Heineken Music Hall
Arena Boulevard 590, Bijlmermeer.
0900 687 4242. www.heineken-
music-hall.nl.
Famed for having the best accoustics in Europe, the Heineken Music Hall is a mammoth venue in an out-of-town location—you'll need to take the metro to get here if you don't have a car. Recent pop artists performing here have included Avril Lavigne, Limp Bizkit and Ricky Martin.

Paradiso
Weteringschans 6, Canals Area.
020 626 4521. www.paradiso.nl.
Housed in a converted church, the Paradiso is a much-loved venue among touring international and national musicians as well as locals. Headline acts performing here in the past have included Kelis, The Strokes, and Neneh Cherry. When there's no live band, there are usually DJs playing, with popular club nights including cheesy 1990s classics.

NIGHTLIFE

133

RESTAURANTS

A wide variety of food is served in the Netherlands, from local dishes to international cuisine. The country's colonial past helps explain why Asia is represented particularly well, especially when it comes to Indonesian restaurants. Chinese, Japanese, Indian and fusion restaurants are also not difficult to find. Generally speaking, Dutch restaurants are not large establishments, and consequently they can fill up quickly at lunchtime and early evening. It makes sense to reserve a table if a meal is to be a special occasion.

Prices and Hours

The restaurants below were selected for their ambience, location, typical dishes or unusual character. Prices are based on the cost of an appetizer, entrée and dessert for one person, without beverage, tax or tip. Most restaurants are open daily (except where noted). Lunch is usually served 11am–2:30pm or 3pm and dinner 5:30pm–10pm or 11pm. Not all accept major credit cards. *The following legend indicates the price ranges for the restaurants described.*

$ <21 euros
$$ 21–35 euros
$$$ 35–55 euros
$$$$ >55 euros

Dutch Cuisine

Any mention of typical Dutch dishes must include **seafood** like *haring* (raw herring), *Zeeuwse oesters* and *Zeeuwse mosselen* (oysters and mussels from Zeeland), *gerookte paling* (smoked eel), and *kibbeling* (deep-fried breaded white fish). To eat herring the traditional way, hold the fish by the tail and let it slip down your throat. Herring does not have to be eaten raw; preserved in vinegar and herbs, **pickled herring**, known as *zure haring*, is available year round.

Meat-based dishes lie at the heart of Dutch cuisine; pork, beef and chicken are staples in most restaurants. *Rookvlees*, for example, is a thinly sliced smoked **beef** that is typically served on a slice of buttered bread. **Sausages** are popular, usually as snacks: *ossenworst*, for example, is a beef sausage, served either raw or smoked, with mustard. *Gelderse rookworst* is a smoked pork sausage from Gelderland. A more acquired taste is *balkenbrij*— similar to black pudding—made from whatever is left from a butchered pig.

Dutch **breads** are wholesome and tasty. White bread is still popular, though brown breads and French-style varieties have become more common. Rye bread (*roggebrood*) is often available and comes in a coarse, black variety as well as a drier version from Limburg and Brabant in the south. Spiced cake is made in various forms: with nuts, raisins or orange peel. Deventer honey cake (*Deventer koek*) takes its name from the town where the bread has been made since the late 16C.

The Netherlands is famous for its **cheeses**. Gouda is available as young, ripe, mature and extra-mature: the flavors are quite distinct; there is no mistaking the

Parmesan-like taste of extra-mature Gouda with the creamy mildness of its younger counterpart. Seek out goat cheese, *boerenkaas* (farmer's cheese), cumin-flavored cheese, and *nagelkaas*, which is made with cloves.

Must-Try Dishes

Dishes to look out for include **stamppot**, mashed potatoes with either kale or sauerkraut typically served with a Dutch sausage; and **zuurvlees**, a meat-based stew from the south of the country. *Pannenkoeken* (**pancakes**) are always an affordable and filling meal, with specialist pancake houses selling both savory and sweet varieties. Usually prepared in a shallow copper pan, **poffertjes** are small fluffy pancakes topped with butter and powdered sugar.

Old Amsterdam

De Bakkerswinkel
$ International
Zeedijk 37. 020 489 8000. www.bakkerswinkel.nl.
This cozy lunchroom offers soups, salads, sandwiches, sweets and more on its adorably decorated menu. Fresh-baked, crusty bread is the basis of its deluxe sandwiches, stuffed with quality meats and local cheese; finish off lunch with one of the irresistible pies, cakes or pastries that beckon from the display. Closed dinner.

Café Bern
$ Swiss
Nieuwmarkt 9. 020 622 0034. Dinner only. Cash only.
What looks and feels like a quintessential Dutch *bruin cafe* (a traditional Dutch pub) is actually

one of the city's favorite spots for the Swiss specialty of fondue. Locals stop by chiefly for the restaurant's star trifecta of molten cheese, crusty bread and red wine. Reservations recommended.

Oriental City
$ Chinese
Oudezijds Voorburgwal 177. 020 626 9295. www.oriental-city.nl.
The multistorey Oriental City, on the corner of Damstraat, feels like a typical Chinese banquet hall, and offers a comfortable perch from which diners can people-watch. Cantonese favorites and a few Sichuan choices fill the menu, but the dim sum *(daily 11:30am–5pm)* is the star of the show.

La Place
$ International
Kalverstraat 203. 0900 235 8363. www.laplace.nl.
Self-service restaurant chain La Place offers sandwiches and salads, savory omelets, decadent pies and more, with drinks from fresh-squeezed juices to Fair Trade coffee. From their location on the top floor of Vroom & Dreesman department store, most any La Place in the country will have a stellar view of its respective city.

Thai Bird
$ Thai
Zeedijk 72–74. 020 620 1442. www.thai-bird.nl. Dinner only.
This popular eatery in Amsterdam's Chinatown is always packed, so expect to stand in line if you don't have a reservation. Try classics like the lamb *massaman*, which is rich, sweet and meaty—or vegetarian takes on traditional dishes, such as the tofu in red curry.

Dine Out at Home

Dine with the Dutch (www.dinewiththedutch.com) pairs tourists with a Dutch family who welcomes them into their house for a home-cooked, three-course dinner. Diners see firsthand how the Dutch eat, and chat with their hosts about life in the Netherlands. The leisurely meal lasts three to four hours, and costs €50 per adult, €35 for children 4 to12 years old.

Huiskamerrestaurants are ad-hoc "restaurants" set up in private residences, where amateur chefs serve a *table d'hote* menu from their home kitchen, while diners strike up a camaraderie at the communal table.

One of the first such restaurants, **Saskia's Huiskamer** (*Albert Cuypstraat 203; 062 863 9839; www.huiskamerrestaurant.com*) is now a full-time catering business, but invites smaller parties to one open dinner per month (reservations required). For other huiskamerrestaurants, access *www.livingroommenu.com*.

Haesje Claes
$$ **Dutch**
Spuistraat 269. 020 624 9998.
www.haesjeclaes.nl.
The decor is as old-fashioned as the spelling of this traditional Dutch restaurant's name. The food is simple, but portions are generous and excellent value for money. Try one of the seasonal *stamppotten* (see *Cuisine above*).

Hofje van Wijs
$$ **Dutch**
Zeedijk 43. 020 624 0436.
www.wijs-zonen.nl. Closed Mon.
This coffee and tea "Purveyor to the Queen," in business for over 200 years, now serves traditional Dutch favorites from its Chinatown location. Dishes such as *hachee* (a richly spiced stew from Brabant), mussels from Zeeland (in season) and the Dutch dessert sampler can be washed down with beer from Amsterdam brewery De Prael.

Kantjil & De Tijger
$$ **Indonesian**
Spuistraat 291-293. 020 620 0994.
www.kantjil.nl.
Something of an Amsterdam institution, Kantjil & de Tijger has the feel of a large Indonesian canteen. The decor is bright and a little spartan, but service is speedy and the menu extensive. Try an Indonesian *rijsttafel* (literally meaning "rice table") for a good selection of dishes to share.

Restaurant Tibet
$$ **Tibetan**
Lange Niezel 24. 020 624 1137.
www.tibet-restaurant.nl.
Amid the tourist traps of De Walletjes, Restaurant Tibet welcomes visitors into a colorful, homey atmosphere to sample cuisine from the roof of the world. Savory *momos* (Tibetan

Hofje van Wijs
©Hofje van Wijs

potstickers), assorted stews and stir-fries and Chinese Sichuan dishes appear on the quirkily worded menu.

De Roode Leeuw
$$ Dutch
In Hotel Amsterdam, Damrak 93. 020 555 0666. www.restaurant deroodeleeuw.nl.
This brasserie on the busy street running south from Centraal Station serves Dutch specialties such as *kapucijners*: a type of bean (between a kidney bean and chickpea) served with bacon and onion. The restaurant also prepares classic *Noord-Hollandse erwtensoep* (pea soup) with smoked sausage.

D'Vijff Vlieghen
$$$ Dutch
Spuistraat 294–302. 020 530 4060. www.vijffvlieghen.nl. Dinner only.
Expect high-end Dutch cooking in an atmospheric, typically Amsterdam setting. The restaurant is housed in a building so old it slants disturbingly to one side. Inside are a jumble of rooms all beautifully decorated in 17C style.

In de Waag
$$$ Mediterranean
Nieuwmarkt 4. 020 422 7772. www.indewaag.nl.
This pleasant cafe-restaurant sits in the city's historic weigh-house *(waag)*. The menu emphasizes fish, all of which is certified by the Marine Stewardship Council for its sustainability, and organic artisanal products. There is also a wine bar, a reading table and a large terrace in summer.

Supperclub
$$$$ International
Jonge Roelensteeg 21. 020 344 6400. www.supperclub.com. Dinner only.
A not-to-be-missed experience, the Supperclub is as much about being entertained as dining. Customers lounge on enormous white beds, and enjoy performances of anything from cabaret to drag acts during the evening. The restaurant offers a five-course surprise menu with an eclectic mix of food.

The Canals

Japanese Pancake World
$ Japanese
Tweede Egelantiersdwarsstraat 24A. 020 320 4447. www.japanese pancakeworld.com.
Japanese food in Amsterdam is usually either mediocre or extraordinary; Japanese Pancake World, a specialist in *okonomiyaki*, is unquestionably the latter. The menu has several variations on this savory dish from Osaka, a cross between a pancake and an omelet, topped with paper-thin bonito flakes and cross-hatched with special sauces.

Pancake Bakery
$ Dutch
Prinsengracht 191. 020 625 13 33. www.pancake.nl.
This pancake restaurant, close to Anne Frank Huis, offers 75 different sweet and savory pancakes in both typical Dutch and international varieties amid quaintly traditional decor. The cheese pancakes, loaded with optional extras, are a favorite, as are the bite-size *poffertjes*, the Dutch version of silver-dollar pancakes.

RESTAURANTS

BIHP

$$ **Mediterranean**

*Keizersgracht 335. 020 622 4511.
www.bihp.nl. Dinner only.
Closed Sun and Mon.*

Sophisticated yet informal,
BIHP offers a modern, intimate
ambience in an ideal canal-side
location. The menu is largely
Mediterranean influenced, with
favorites like the Greek Orzo main
and the Sgroppino dessert. The
art work on the walls is worth a
second look, too.

Cous Cousine

$$ **North African**

*Westerstraat 40. 020 625 2756.
www.couscousine.nl. Dinner only.*
North Africa meets Asia in this
fusion of culinary cultures. Expect
creative takes on tagines, and a
veritable medley of Moroccan and
Indian spices to adorn your plate.
The decor leans towards North
African, and the service is friendly
and attentive.

Indrapura

$$ **Indonesian**

*Rembrandtplein 40-42. 020 623
7329. www.indrapura.nl.*
This restaurant on lively
Rembrandtplein serves excellent
renditions of such Indonesian
classics as *loempia* (fried rolls),

Indrapura
©indrapura

sate (skewered meat with peanut
sauce) and piquant *sambals* (chili
sauces), as well as the Indonesian
banquet dinner *rijsttafel*.

Memories of India

$$ **Indian**

*Reguliersdwarsstraat 88. 020 623
5710. www.memoriesofindia.nl.
Dinner only.*
Good Indian food is not easy to
come by in Amsterdam, but this
restaurant is an exception. Though
the food is more expensive than
competitors', the decor is smarter
and the dishes are a cut above. Try
the fresh and spicy prawn *biryani*
or the salty, iron-rich flavors of
paneer cheese in spinach sauce.

De Struisvogel

$$ **French**

*Keizersgracht 312. 020 423 3817.
www.restaurantdestruisvogel.nl.
Dinner only.*
This cozy basement restaurant
with dark wood features is perfect
for a winter's evening. *Struisvogel*
literally means ostrich, and it is the
restaurant's specialty. The menu
is simple, usually offering three
starters, three mains and three
desserts, with fish and vegetarian
options for those who aren't into
ostrich.

Tempo Doeloe

$$ **Indonesian**

*Utrechtsestraat 75. 020 625 6718.
www.tempodoeloerestaurant.nl.
Dinner only.*
Known for being one of the best
Indonesian restaurants in town,
Tempo Doeloe translates as "the
good old days in the past." A
reservation is a must, as diners
regularly wait for tables. Here, the
rijsttafel (literally "rice table": a

selection of small dishes to share) comes on three platters: mild, spicy and hot. Beware the hot dishes, as they certainly live up to their reputation.

XINH
$$ **Vietnamese**
Elandsgracht 2. 020 624 0308. www.xinh.nl. Dinner only. Closed Mon.

Vietnamese restaurants are still few in Amsterdam, and an excellent bowl of phở, Vietnam's national noodle soup, was hard to find until Xinh opened in the Jordaan. Favorites like phở, rolls (*cuốn*) and Vietnamese iced coffee, laced with syrupy condensed milk, are offered, as well as an unusually broad wine menu.

Bordewijk
$$$ **French**
Noordermarkt 7. 020 624 3899. www.bordewijk.nl. Dinner only. Closed Sun and Mon.

A contemporary French restaurant with an excellent reputation, Bordewijk is an accessible entry into fine dining. The kitchen focuses on local, seasonal produce—especially game when in season—with the menu changing regularly.

Castell
$$$ **Barbecue**
Lijnbaansgracht 253-254. 020 622 8606. www.castellamsterdam.nl. Dinner only.

One of the few barbecue restaurants in the city is doing a roaring trade in lamb cutlets, succulent steaks, huge racks of marinated ribs and great side dishes, including baked jacket potatoes (which are surprisingly

hard to find in Amsterdam), coleslaw and salads. Castell is one of only a handful of places serving food up until midnight.

Kinnaree
$$$ **Thai**
Eerste Anjeliersdwarsstraat 14. 020 627 7153. www.restaurant kinnaree.nl. Dinner only.

With a fresh, modern interior, Kinnaree has few of the trappings of typically kitsch Thai establishments. Located in the heart of the Jordaan, the restaurant offers all the usual Thai suspects plus a few more modern, creative dishes. The seared duck breast with peppercorns and garlic comes highly recommended.

La Oliva
$$$ **Spanish**
Egelantiersstraat 122. 020 320 4316. www.laoliva.nl.

La Oliva specializes in fine Spanish wines and *pintxos*, which is a catch-all Basque term for the small, made-to-share finger food that's often served with drinks, much like tapas. Lined up along the bar, most of the *pintxos* come on bread, topped with anything from foie gras to grilled vegetables. This intimate restaurant also serves a regular à la carte menu, though it tends to be pricey.

Utrechtsedwarstafel
$$$$ **International**
Utrechtsedwarsstraat 107-109. 020 625 4189. www.utrechtsedwarstafel.com. Dinner only. Closed Sun, Mon and Tue.

Chef and sommelier come together to create this restaurant's concept: *wijn en spijs*, the pairing

of wines with flavors. The chef buys his produce daily and puts together a surprise menu based on what's in season, organic and available. While prices are high, they do include parings with food.

The Ports

Bickers aan de Werf
$$ **International**
Bickerswerf 2. 020 320 2951. www.bickersaandewerf.nl.
Right on the water to the west of Centraal Station, Bickers feels a world away from the bustle of the city center. The large terrace is a great spot for a late afternoon glass of wine. Sandwiches and salads are available during the day, while the dinner menu is international and varied.

De Gouden Reael
$$ **French**
Zandhoek 14. 020 623 3883. www.goudenreael.nl. Dinner only.
Superbly situated on the old harbor, De Gouden Reael offers a bistro-style menu of French local dishes that change every two months. Expect classic meat preparations, including charcuterie, country-style pâté and steak tartare, as well as *salade niçoise* and for non-meat eaters, warm goat cheese salad.

Open
$$ **Mediterranean**
Westerdoksplein 20. 020 620 1010. www.open.nl.
Housed in what looks like an enormous pod suspended above the westerly dock, this restaurant has a modern, trendy vibe to it, with great outdoor space in summer. The Med-led menu changes frequently, with the daily specials usually a good choice.

Greetje
$$$ **Dutch**
Peperstraat 23-25. 020 779 7450. www.restaurantgreetje.nl. Dinner only. Closed Mon. Reservations required.
Traditional Dutch food is given a new lease on life at this local favorite, which is at its cozy best in winter. Try the venison stew and old-fashioned bread pudding. Prices are on the high side, but the service is excellent.

Sea Palace
$$$ **Chinese**
Oosterdokskade 8. 020 626 4777. www.seapalace.nl.
This iconic Chinese restaurant actually floats on the water just east of Centraal Station. Its novelty factor is a clear hit with families with children. With a great view across the water toward city center, Sea Palace justifies prices that cash in on location. The extensive menu specializes in Cantonese dishes.

Fifteen
$$$$ **Italian**
Jollemanhof 9. 020 509 5015. www.fifteen.nl. No lunch Sun.
British celebrity chef Jamie Oliver's spacious restaurant serves

Fifteen
©ATCB

Italian seasonal classics with a contemporary flair. The menu, which rotates biweekly, marries local meats, seafood and produce with imported Italian delicacies for the best of both worlds.

De Pijp

Bazar
$ **North African**
Albert Cuypstraat 182. 020 675 0544. www.bazaramsterdam.nl.
A huge, split-level affair, Bazar looks like it has been decorated as just that: colored glass "chandeliers," mosaic tiles and intricate paintwork all add to the ambience of a Middle Eastern bazaar. The food is Moroccan in flavor, with a wide choice of mezze-style dishes to start and kebab- and couscous-based main courses.

Braque
$$ **French**
Albert Cuypstraat 29-31. 020 670 7357. www.caferestaurantbraque. com. Dinner only. Closed Mon.
A relative newcomer to Amsterdam's restaurant scene, Braque has the feel of a traditional French bistro, but with a modern twist. The menu follows suit: classics like *confit de canard* and *steak frites* abound, although the meat can be under-seasoned for some diners' tastes.

District V
$$ **Mediterranean**
Van der Helstplein 17. 020 770 0884. www.district5.nl. Dinner only. Closed Tue.
Tucked in the corner of a leafy square in De Pijp, District V lets its tables spill outside in summer,

giving the restaurant a French-boulevard feel. The menu is simple, featuring three starters, three mains and three desserts, all of which change regularly. French- and Italian-inspired meat, fish and vegetarian options are always available.

De Duvel
$$ **International**
Eerste Van der Helststraat 59-61. 020 675 7517. www.deduvel.nl. No lunch Mon.
This eatery looks like a slightly upscale version of a Dutch *eetcafe*: the decor is simple and cozy, and regular staples like chicken satay with chips are likely to be found on the menu. However, more adventurous dishes, including Italian carpaccio and risottos as well as Asian noodles, are also offered.

Firma Pekelhaaring
$$ **Italian**
Van Woustraat 127-129. 020 679 0460. www.pekelhaaring.nl.
With sort of a retro feel, Firma (or Fa, for short) Pekelhaaring combines well-executed Italian dishes with a vibe that attracts creative local types. The *porchetta* is an absolute must-try dish, served with the best home-made pork sausages in Amsterdam. The antipasti and *vitello tonnato* are also worth the trip.

L'Ozio
$$ **Italian**
Ferdinand Bolstraat 26. 020 470 8183. www.ozioamsterdam.com. No lunch Sun. Closed Mon.
With white, minimalist walls and spartan tableware, L'Ozio is a far cry from the green-and-red

RESTAURANTS

141

pizzerias found elsewhere. The kitchen's stand-out dish is the pasta with wild boar, but since the menu changes every month you may need to ask if you don't see it listed.

South Side

Cobra

$ **International**
Hobbemastraat 18. 020 470 0111. www.cobracafe.nl. Lunch only.
Everything about this cafe-restaurant is inspired by the Cobra art movement *(see Museums)*: the artwork on the walls, the chairs, even the floor and the wine labels. The tableware was designed by Corneille, founding member of the movement. In the summer months, a sushi bar, shop and a large terrace are open.

Hap-Hmm

$ **Dutch**
Eerste Helmersstraat 33. 020 618 1884. www.hap-hmm.nl. Dinner only. Closed Sat and Sun.
This unpretentious eatery, north of Vondelpark, has provided Dutch comfort food to its patrons since 1935. The house specialty of stewed beef is served with two sides and starts at an economical €7.50—a true rarity in the Dutch restaurant world.

Tomatillo

$ **Mexican**
Overtoom 261. 020 683 3086. www.tomatillo.nl. Closed Mon.
For a taste of the Mexican borderlands, look no farther than Tomatillo, whose overstuffed burritos and namesake salsas have wowed Tex-Mex-starved Amsterdammers. For those who prefer their beans for brunch, try the delectable *huevos rancheros*. Seating is limited, but with Vondelpark down the block, it's the ideal set-up for an *alfresco* meal.

Blauw

$$$ **Indonesian**
Amstelveenseweg 158-160. 020 675 5000. www.restaurantblauw. nl. Dinner only.
A split-level space full of reds and blues, Blauw is not your typical Indonesian eatery. The *rijsttafel* (literally "rice table," a selection of small dishes to share) comes highly recommended. Desserts are also uncharacteristically good for this type of cuisine. The Amstelveenseweg is an up-and-coming neighborhood in terms of restaurants and bars, so if Blauw is full, be sure to check out some of its local competitors.

Le Garage

$$$ **French**
Ruysdaelstraat 54-56. 020 679 7176. www.restaurantlegarage.nl. No lunch Sat and Sun.
This modern brasserie boasts a great reputation and an artsy atmosphere, making it a hot spot for 🚗 **celebrity sightings**. The owner's appearances on Dutch television only add to its star quality. The menu offers brasserie fare, such as snails and bouillabaisse, and classic French desserts, like *île flottante*.

🚗 Ron Blaauw

$$$$ **International**
Sophialaan 55. 020 496 1943. www.ronblaauw.nl. No lunch Sat. Closed Sun and Mon.
One of Holland's premier chefs, Ron Blaauw recently moved his

restaurant from several miles south of the city to the heart of wealthy Amsterdam South. His creative, fine-dining cuisine has earned him high ratings in the past, but the restaurant has none of the stuffy pretentiousness of some upscale establishments.

Yamazato
$$$$ **Japanese**
In Hotel Okura, Ferdinand Bolstraat 333. 020 678 8351. www.yamazato.nl.
Perched on the top floor (*23rd*) of Hotel Okura, this Japanese restaurant, recognized for its culinary excellence, introduces diners to the art of *kaiseki*, or traditional Japanese haute cuisine. The multi-course set meals feature seasonal, ocean-fresh fish prepared with the utmost delicacy. Sushi and sashimi can be ordered à la carte.

Outside City Center

Hotel de Goudfazant
$$ **Mediterranean**
Aambeeldstraat 10. 020 636 5170. www.hoteldegoudfazant.nl. Dinner only. Closed Mon.
In Amsterdam North, on the opposite side of the water from Centraal Station, sits the Hotel de Goudfazant, in what appears to be an industrial estate.
A restaurant rather than a hotel, the Goudfazant has an airy warehouse feel, coupled with a bustling pace. In summer, diners can enjoy generous, seasonal Mediterranean dishes outside overlooking the IJ.

De Kas
$$$ **International**
Kamerlingh Onneslaan 3. 020 462 4562. www.restaurantdekas.nl. Closed Sun.
Kas means greenhouse in Dutch, and this restaurant's enormous glasshouse is home not only to the dining area, but also to huge flowerbeds growing organic fruit, vegetables and herbs. All other ingredients used by the kitchen are sourced from nearby farms. Vegetarians are well catered to here, and can be assured of minimal time between field and plate.

Nomads
$$$ **Lebanese**
Rozengracht 133. 020 344 6401. www.nomads.nl. Dinner only.
A real concept restaurant, Nomads is all about experience: diners take their shoes off to sit cross-legged on large piles of Middle Eastern rugs, while being served mezze-style food on silver platters by svelte, bare-chested waiters. The food is better than average, but expect to pay for the wow factor.

 Vis aan de Schelde
$$$ **Seafood**
Scheldeplein 4. 020 675 1583. www.visaandeschelde.nl. Closed 2 weeks late Dec–early Jan.
One of Amsterdam's best-kept fish secrets, Vis aan de Schelde occupies an unassuming position beside a roundabout en route to the RAI. Fresh oysters are always on the menu, and the kitchen does an excellent line in surf 'n turf entrées, such as seared haddock and scallops with pata negra ham and black venus rice.

HOTELS

Amsterdam offers a wide range of accommodations, even including houseboats, to suit every budget and comfort level. The city's luxury, high-end hotels are mainly concentrated in and around the old center, along the canal belt and in the southwest, close to Vondelpark and the major museums. By contrast, De Pijp in the south is home to some smaller, less expensive hotels and B&B guesthouses. Farther out of town, the hotels tend to be more affordable and have higher availability, if you are willing to overnight away from the city center.

Prices and Amenities

Amsterdam is known for its high lodging costs compared to the rest of the Netherlands, so expect to pay capital-city prices wherever you stay. On the plus side, whether you choose a budget hostel or a luxury hotel, the staff is sure to speak excellent English. Unless otherwise noted, prices are based on a double room for one night in high season, not including taxes or surcharges. Most all properties accept major credit cards. Many have non-smoking rooms. Numerous hotels featured in this guide provide Internet access and several have excellent restaurants. *The following legend indicates price ranges for the lodgings described.*

$ <70 euros
$$ 70-100 euros
$$$ 100-140 euros
$$$$ 140-200 euros
$$$$$ >200 euros

Online Booking

Accommodations should be reserved in advance as far as possible, especially for weekends in spring and summer.
The more picturesque hotels along the canals fill up fast, so early booking is a must. The Amsterdam Tourism & Convention Board maintains an online hotel directory and reservations service at www.iamsterdam.com. A wide range of lodgings can be reserved through **Booking.com**, which offers an online reservations service at www.booking.com/city/nl/amsterdam.html, or call 020 712 5600.

Search Engines

For urban hostels, visit Hostelling International's website: www.hihostels.com. Information and online booking is also available at www.stayokay.com. Bed and breakfast-style inns can be found through Bed & Breakfast Nederland online at www.bedandbreakfast.nl, (31) 049 733 0300.

Hotels on Maps

The accommodations are listed in this section under Amsterdam's major districts. On maps in this guide, hotels are numbered to correspond with the legend that accompanies each map.
Some lodgings may appear on the maps on the inside covers.

Old Amsterdam

Shelter City Hostel

$ **176 beds**
Barndesteeg 21. 020 625 3230.
www.shelter.nl.
This nonprofit Christian hostel, located on an alley in the middle

MUST STAY

of the Walletjes, seems a paradox; nevertheless, its communal atmosphere and deep-rooted philosophy make it an attractively different destination for Christian and non-Christian travelers alike. Both dormitories and private rooms are available. The €15.50 per person per night includes breakfast.

Stayokay Amsterdam Stadsdoelen

$ **170 beds**

Kloveniersburgwal 97. 020 624 6832. www.stayokay.com/ stadsdoelen.

Part of a chain in the Netherlands, this hostel is the most central of the three in Amsterdam. Near the red-light district, and a stone's throw from Dam square, its canal-side location is very convenient for busy backpackers. Minimum stay of two nights required on Saturdays. Shared (unisex and mixed) and private rooms available. Shared showers and toilets. The €35.50 per person per night rate includes breakfast.

Hotel Amsterdam

$$$ **79 rooms**

Damrak 93. 020 555 0666. www.hotelamsterdam.nl.

This hotel offers well appointed rooms in an historic building in the heart of the city, steps from Dam square. Amsterdam's leading department store, De Bijenkorf, is located opposite the hotel. Restaurant De Roode Leeuw *(see Restaurants)* serves regional specialties and international dishes for lunch and dinner, making use of the terrace in good weather. Minimum stay two nights. Breakfast included in the rate.

Hotel Estheréa

$$$ **92 rooms**

Singel 303-309. 020 624 5146. www.estherea.nl.

From both inside and out, Hotel Estheréa preserves the look and feel of an upper-class 17C canal house; its water-side location in the Nieuwe Zijde puts it close to Dam square and other central attractions. Patrons can make use of the hotel fitness center and a library stocked with international newspapers.

Hotel Estheréa

©Hotel Estheréa

The Convent Hotel Amsterdam

$$$$ **148 rooms**

Nieuwezijds Voorburgwal 67. 020 627 5900. www.mgallery.com/gb/ hotel-1159-the-convent-hotel- amsterdam/index.shtml.

It's not unusual for an Amsterdam hotel to occupy a monumental canal house, but the Convent Hotel's premises are certainly unique, as the former site of two medieval monasteries and much later, a major Dutch newspaper. Inside, the modern high-end hotel offers amenities such as a fitness center and sauna.

The Grand

$$$$ **182 rooms**

Oudezijds Voorburgwal 197. 020 555 3111. www.thegrand.nl.

This well-regarded hotel, a Sofitel

property, is housed in the former Prinsenhof dating to the 16C when the Dutch Royal Family were frequent visitors. Luxury quarters overlook the canal or the inner courtyard. A gourmet restaurant, Bridges, various lounges and bars, and spa facilities (indoor heated pool, Jacuzzi, Turkish steam bath, sauna and fitness equipment) are added pluses.

Hotel Nes
$$$$ **39 rooms**
Kloveniersburgwal 137. 020 624 4773. www.hotelnes.nl.
This environmentally friendly hotel resides in a traditional canal house. Located in the center of Amsterdam, it is just a few minutes' walk from Centraal Station, Kalverstraat shopping, and the buzzing restaurants and bars of Rembrantplein and Nieuwmarkt. Hotel Nes provides simply furnished rooms, with some offering canal views. It also has a cozy lounge with a fireplace. Breakfast included.

NH Grand Hotel Krasnapolsky
$$$$ **468 rooms**
Dam 9. 020 554 9111. www.nh-hotels.com/NHKrasnapolsky.
Travelers would be hard-pressed to find a more peaceful retreat in a more central location. The ritzy hotel flanks the eastern perimeter of Dam square. It boasts several dining spots: the historic Winter Garden for a deluxe breakfast buffet (€28.50); for dinner, the French-Dutch Restaurant Reflet and Grand Cafe Mathildé (both €36). Use of the fitness center is included in the rate.

Hotel de l'Europe
$$$$$ **100 rooms**
Nieuwe Doelenstraat 2-14. 020 531 1777. www.leurope.nl.
This famous hotel of Victorian grandeur is close to Muntplein. The new Dutch Masters Wing, opened in 2010, houses an annex of 23 suites, each featuring a replica painting from the Rijksmuseum. The Excelsior restaurant, known for its outstanding wine cellar, has a unusual view of the Amstel River. The hotel also has a heated indoor pool, solarium and fitness club. Breakfast is included in the rate.

The Canals

NL Hotel
$$$ **13 rooms**
Nassaukade 368. 020 689 0030. www.nl-hotel.com.
Located in the center of Amsterdam, minutes from lively Leidseplein, this new and trendy boutique hotel offers modern, well-appointed rooms. Amsterdam's prime entertainment district, museums, restaurants and shopping areas are a short walk away. As extra services, the hotel can arrange bike rentals, boat trips and the use of a laptop or prepaid mobile phone.

Seven Bridges Hotel
$$$ **8 rooms**
Reguliersgracht 31. 020 623 1329. www.sevenbridgeshotel.nl.
Old World finery is the trademark of this 1710 canal house, filled with a treasure trove of antiques from the Baroque, Louis XV, Louis XVI, Empire, Biedermeier and Art Deco periods. The hotel offers free Wi-Fi and local calls. The optional breakfast (€12.50) is served, characteristically, on fine china.

The Toren
$$$ **38 rooms**
Keizersgracht 164. 020 622 6352.
www.thetoren.nl.
The timeless 17C exterior of
The Toren ("The Tower") pairs
splendidly with its contemporary-
classic interior decor. While each
of the guest rooms has its own
atmosphere, the hotel is unified
in its impression of luxurious
comfort and tranquility. Guests can
order room service from French
restaurant Christophe', thanks to a
partnership between the hotel and
restaurant.

Ambassade
$$$$ **58 rooms**
Herengracht 341. 020 555 0222.
www.ambassade-hotel.nl.
This stylish hotel is superbly
located within a group of 17C
houses on the Herengracht, close
to the tourist center. The decor of
the rooms and communal areas
juxtaposes antique furniture with
modern paintings from the famous
Cobra movement *(see Museums)*.
The hotel offers its own Float &
Massage Center.

American
$$$$ **175 rooms**
Leidsekade 97. 020 556 3000.
www.edenamsterdamamerican
hotel.com.
Just off the Leidseplein, the well-
known American Hotel, a member
of the Eden group, is famous for
its Art Deco interior. Originally
built in 1900, the hotel became
popular in the "Roaring Twenties"
and has retained something of
that vibe since. Its magnificent
cafe-restaurant is often frequented
by politicians and leading figures
in the arts, making it a great place

to people-watch over coffee.
Breakfast, lunch and dinner are
available, and the hotel also has a
sauna and fitness facilities.

Renaissance Amsterdam Hotel
$$$$ **402 rooms**
Kattengat 1. 020 621 2223. www.
renaissanceamsterdamhotel.com.
The Renaissance occupies a
handy location near Centraal
Station, a 10min walk from Dam
square. Renovated guest rooms
have modern furnishings and a
seating area, and some rooms
grant access to a special lounge
with complimentary breakfast
and snack services. The hotel
fitness center is open 24hrs a
day. For drinks, snacks and meals,
seek out the 2B lounge bar and
Mediterranean restaurant Scossa.
The Koepelcafé serves drinks and
meals throughout the day.

Synopsis Hotel
$$$$ **3 rooms**
Nieuwe Keizersgracht 22-A. 020
626 0075. www.synopsishotel.com.
This diminutive boutique hotel bills
itself as "the smallest luxury hotel
in the center of Amsterdam," but it's
quality, not quantity, that propels
the demand for its three lavish
rooms. Free wireless Internet is
available in all rooms; the spacious
Courtyard hotel room has a private
patio. The rate includes breakfast.

Seven One Seven
$$$$$ **8 rooms**
Prinsengracht 717. 020 427 0717.
www.717hotel.nl.
Housed in a grand, atmospheric,
19C building along the canal
Prinsengracht, this boutique hotel
offers an all-inclusive formula.
Afternoon tea, drinks from the

mini-bar and a selection of house wines are complimentary. Breakfast (included in the rate) is served in your room, in the bright breakfast area, or on the patio during summer. You may smoke in the library and relax with an in-room spa treatment.

Canal House
$$$$$ **23 rooms**
Keizersgracht 148-152. 020 622 5182. www.canalhouse.nl.
This elegant 17C boutique hotel is full of antiques. Furnished individually, each room retains original features like an ornate fireplace, traditional porcelain washstand, timber beams, and the rich, dark colors of old Dutch paintings. A complimentary breakfast is served in the dining room overlooking the garden; an all-day menu is available from the bar and restaurant.

The Dylan
$$$$$ **41 rooms**
Keizersgracht 384. 020 530 2010. www.dylanamsterdam.com.
This boutique hotel along the Keizersgracht is situated in the heart of the canal belt. The Dylan offers rooms and suites with special themes. All have luxurious bathrooms, and guests are provided with a bathrobe and slippers. The hotel includes a lounge/bar area, fitness center, massage service and garden with a terrace. The Dylan's restaurant is located in an 18C bakery with garden views and an excellent wine cellar.

Pulitzer
$$$$$ **230 rooms**
Prinsengracht 315-331. 020 523 5235. www.hotelpulitzeramsterdam.nl.

This magnificent hotel in the heart of the canal belt was created from 25 restored 17C and 18C canal houses. Spacious guest rooms have views over the canal, inner courtyard or gardens. The decor is modern with classic Dutch character. Keizersgracht 238, the hotel's restaurant, is well known in the city, specializing in locally sourced grilled meat and fish. The hotel also has an art gallery and a gym.

The Ports

🛏 Amstel Botel
$$ **175 rooms**
NDSM Pier 3. 020 626 4247. www.amstelbotel.com.
Moored near a former shipyard, just north of Centraal Station on the IJ river, this floating "boat hotel" is one of the largest of its kind. Rooms are well-appointed and overlook either the land or water side (the latter being slightly more expensive). The hotel has a bar and reception area. Minimum two nights' stay required if a Saturday is booked.

🛏 Lloyd Hotel
$$ **117 rooms**
Oostelijke Handelskade 34. 020 561 3636. www.lloydhotel.com.
Housed in a renovated 1920s building, the Lloyd offers a range of sleeping quarters from rooms with a shared bathroom to luxurious suites. All include original features; some boast modern Dutch designer furniture. Located in the Eastern Docklands, the hotel features a cultural embassy with free events, a spacious street terrace and a library. Sandwiches and light meals are served in

Lloyd Hotel

©Allard van der Hoek/Lloyd Hotel

the restaurant, which focuses on carefully sourced ingredients. A shop sells delicatessen-style foods and designer gifts.

Westcord Art Hotel
$$$ 130 rooms
Spaarndammerdijk 304. 020 410 9670. www.westcordhotels.com.
The hotel is slightly outside the city center, but easily accessible from Centraal Station via a 10min bus ride. Its location makes it convenient to drive to, given the relative proximity of the A10 ring road. Common areas are filled with various art, and the hotel has its own restaurant and cafe, The Gallery and Art Cafe respectively. Open May through August, a swimming pool with free access sits next to the hotel.

Grand Hotel Amrâth
$$$$$ 165 rooms
Prins Hendrikkade 108. 020 552 0000. www.amrathamsterdam.com.
Housed in an impressive Art Deco building that used to be a shipping house, the luxurious Amrâth is full of character. Room interiors feature high ceilings and large windows. An indoor swimming pool and high-tech gym complement an extensive wellness area with saunas, a Turkish steam bath and a whirlpool. Elegant Seven Seas restaurant serves French and international cuisine in the evening. Guests can enjoy drinks, snacks and even high tea in the hotel bar, which is classically decorated with wood-paneled walls.

Mövenpick Hotel
$$$$$ 408 rooms.
Piet Heinkade 11. 020 519 1200. www.moevenpick-hotels.com.
Rising on the edge of the IJ, behind Centraal Station and next to the Muziekgebouw, this hotel offers soundproof rooms with air-conditioning and river views. Guests can make free use of the fitness area, sauna, bio-sauna and unique shower facilities. The Silk Road Restaurant serves an east-meets-west menu; the Silk Bar has an extensive cocktail list and serves snacks and light meals all day.

De Pijp

Bed and Breakfast Parkview
$$ 4 rooms
Sarphatipark 96. 065 568 9769. www.bedandbreakfastpark view.com.
This small B&B overlooking the Sarphatipark occupies a house built in 1855. Each decorated in a different color, rooms vary in size. The largest sleeps four and has a kitchenette and balcony. The second large room sleeps three-four people and has a separate kitchen with its own dining area. The double room is fitted with a kitchenette, but the single room has a microwave and refrigerator. Minimum stay two nights. Breakfast not included in the rate.

HOTELS

Vivaldi Budget Hotel
$$$ **24 rooms**
Stadhouderskade 68. 020 577 6300.
This small, affordable hotel offers
simple, comfortable lodgings.
Its location is both convenient
and unique: close to the city's
popular Vondelpark on one side,
and De Pijp's buzzing bars and
clubs on the other. It is great for
a long weekend of partying by
night and relaxing in the park by
day. Minimum stay two nights.
Breakfast is included in the rate.

Hotel V
$$$$ **48 rooms**
Weteringschans 136. 020 662 3233.
www.hotelv.nl. 48 rooms.
With the canal belt on one side
and De Pijp neighborhood on the
other, Hotel V is well situated for
a long weekend in Amsterdam.
The staff claim to be passionate
about their city, and their mission
is to help guests get the most out
of their stay. Rooms are modern,
with a unique design, and the
atmosphere is young and creative.
The hotel also boasts an intimate
lounge, and a bar where drinks and
snacks are served. Minimum stay of
two nights required at peak times.
Breakfast is included in the rate.

Nicolaas Witsen
$$$$ **28 rooms.**
Nicolaas Witsenstraat 4. 020 623
6143. www.hotelnicolaaswitsen.nl.
A simple but comfortable hotel
on a quiet street, Nicolaas Witsen
is within walking distance
of the main museums and
Rembrandtplein and Leidseplein.
The three buildings that the
hotel occupies were built in
1906, giving them a turn-of-the-
century character. Rooms are well

appointed with free Wi-Fi and
flat-screen TVs. The hotel has a bar
and breakfast room (rate includes
breakfast).

Hotel Okura
$$$$$ **301 rooms**
Ferdinand Bolstraat 333. 020 678
7111. www.okura.nl.
The luxurious Hotel Okura has an
address in trendy De Pijp.
Modern rooms are decorated with
warm colors and have marble
bathrooms. The fitness center
and indoor swimming pool offer
relaxation and recreation. The
hotel's five high-quality restaurants
include the French restaurant Ciel
Bleu and the Japanese restaurant
Yamazato (*see Restaurants*). The
champagne and cocktail bar (*23rd
floor*) offers magnificent views of
Amsterdam.

South Side

Qbic Hotel Amsterdam WTC
$ **55 rooms**
Mathijs Vermeulenpad 1. 043 321
1111. www.qbichotels.com.
The novelty of the Qbic makes
up for its "no-frills" approach: the
"cube" at the core of each room
holds a bed, bathroom, a bar table
with stools, and an LCD TV, all in
one attractive, compact unit. The
hotel also offers free Wi-Fi and an
optional breakfast buffet.

Stayokay Amsterdam Vondelpark
$ **536 beds**
Zandpad 5. 020 589 8996.
www.stayokay.com/vondelpark.
Sitting right in the middle of
Amsterdam's most popular park,
this hostel is the largest and most

modern one in the city. Shared (unisex and mixed) and private rooms are available. All rooms have their own private shower and toilet. A restaurant is available for dinner. Minimum stay two nights if on a Saturday. The €37 per person per night rate includes breakfast.

Borgmann Villa Hotel
$$ **15 rooms**
Koningslaan 48. 020 673 5252. www.hotel-borgmann.nl.
Travelers who prefer a spacious villa to a quaint canal house will feel at home at this mid-quality hotel, which trades in waterside vistas for the landscaped lawns of Vondelpark. It is close to the Museum Quarter and other attractions of South Amsterdam, with excellent transportation connections to city center.

Hotel de Filosoof
$$ **38 rooms**
Anna van den Vondelstraat 6. 020 683 3013. www.sandton.eu/ en/amsterdam.
This hotel is housed in a beautiful 19C building on a quiet street near leafy Vondelpark in south Amsterdam. Reflecting the hotel's name, the decor of its bedrooms and living spaces is based on the thinking of philosophers, such

Hotel de Filosoof
©Hotel de Filosoof

as Wittgenstein, Socrates and Plato. There's also a large garden. Minimum stay two nights.

Aalders
$$$ **28 rooms**
Jan Luijkenstraat 13-15. 020 662 0116. www.hotelaalders.nl.
Sitting on a quiet street, Aalders is a family-run hotel close to the Stedelijk Museum, the Van Gogh Museum and the Rijksmuseum. Simple but comfortable rooms are generally small and cozy. The hotel has an intimate bar and a breakfast room. Minimum stay three nights. Breakfast included in the rate.

Hotel Roemer
©Vondel Hotels

Hotel Roemer
$$$ **23 rooms**
Roemer Visscherstraat 48. 020 515 0453. www.vondelhotels.com.
Old meets new at Hotel Roemer, which offers a selection of ultra-modern amenities—from media centers to iPod docks—in its 18C premises, just footsteps from Vondelpark. The "Roemer Inclusive" rate includes an à la carte breakfast, as well as snacks and drinks.

🏨 Hotel Zandbergen
$$$ **18 rooms**
Willemsparkweg 205. 020 676 9321. www.hotel-zandbergen.com.
The Zandbergen is a small, family-run guesthouse close

to Vondelpark in the Oud Zuid district. The main museums are a 10min walk away. Hotel rooms are small but well appointed. Guests enjoy complimentary tea or coffee on arrival; a continental breakfast (included in the rate) is served every morning. Minimum stay three nights on national holiday weekends.

King's Villa
$$$ **22 rooms**
Koningslaan 64. 020 673 7223.
www.kingsvillahotel.nl.
Overlooking Vondelpark, the King's Villa has a pleasant view from its terrace of the park's small lake. A converted mansion, the hotel building dates to the Art Nouveau era, and the interior is chic but romantic. The hotel has a bar and cozy living room with a fireplace.

Piet Hein
$$$ **80 rooms**
Vossiusstraat 52-53. 020 662 7205.
www.hotelpiethein.nl.
A modern boutique hotel, Piet Hein is right around the corner from Amsterdam's glamorous shopping street, the PC Hooftstraat. But if designer shopping isn't your thing, the hotel is also a stone's throw from popular Vondelpark. Decor is minimalist and trendy, with a nautical twist. Behind the hotel is a garden with a spacious terrace. Breakfast is included in the rate.

College Hotel
$$$$ **40 rooms**
Roelof Hartstraat 1. 020 571 1511.
www.thecollegehotel.com.
This charming boutique hotel is housed in a former school building in fashionable Oud Zuid, within walking distance of the main museums. Rooms are beautifully furnished, and guests can make use of a dressing gown and slippers. The hotel is run by students of the Amsterdam Hotel Management, Catering, and Tourism School, under the eye of experienced professionals. It also offers a gastronomic restaurant where you can dine in style.

Hotel Vondel
$$$$ **86 rooms**
Vondelstraat 18-30. 020 612 0120.
www.vondelhotels.com.
This boutique hotel has a stylish garden terrace in the center of Amsterdam, not far from the Rijksmuseum and Vondelpark. Rooms are spacious, and decorated with contemporary art by Peter Keizer. During warmer weather, breakfast can be enjoyed in the garden. JOOST Eat & Drink serves brasserie-style international cuisine with a selection of Dutch specialties for lunch and dinner. The hotel has a bar serving cocktails. Minimum stay of two nights applies.

Outside City Center

Lucky Lake Hostel
$ **25 caravans, 9 cabins,**
          12 dorm beds
Vinkenkade 75 (Vinkeveen).
029 428 2814. www.luckylake.nl.
Closed end of Sept to Apr.
Outdoorsy and affordable, Lucky Lake takes the hostel concept and spreads it across wooden cabins and caravans (travel trailers) on Vinkeveense Lake; both private "rooms" or four-bed dorms are available, each in its own private cabin or caravan. A private shuttle

transports visitors to the nearest metro station to explore the city. Amenities include bicycle and kayak rental as well as free Wi-Fi. The €19 per person per night rate includes breakfast.

Stayokay Amsterdam Zeeburg
$ 528 beds
Timorplein 21. 020 551 3190.
www.stayokay.com/zeeburg.
Located farther out of the center, in the quieter east of the city, this hostel has its own cafe-restaurant for dinner and shares the premises with interesting neighbors, which means guests don't even have to leave the building to enjoy a movie or theater. It was voted the cleanest hotel 2010 by visitors of hostelsclub.com. Minimum stay two nights if on a Saturday. Shared (unisex and mixed) and private rooms available. Breakfast is included in the rate.

La Casaló
$$ 4 rooms
Amsteldijk 862. 020 642 3680.
This small floating hotel is located right on the river, south of the city, near several parks. Each room is decorated in a different theme: Dutch, Asian, African and Caribbean. You can have breakfast (included in the rate) outside in fine weather.

CitizenM Amsterdam City
$$$ 215 rooms
Prinses Irenestraat 30. 020 811 7090. www.citizenmamsterdam city.com.
South of city center, close to the A10 ring road, CitizenM is easy to access by car or train from Schiphol airport. The hotel offers affordable luxury: innovative interiors, contemporary designer furniture, and modern gadgets like the Philips touch screen MoodPad to control everything in your room from the blinds to the alarm clock. It also boasts its own 24/7 food and drinks outlet, canteenM, where you can buy sandwiches and coffee by day and cocktails and spirits by night.

Arena
$$$$ 116 rooms
's-Gravesandestraat 51. 020 850 2400. www.hotelarena.nl.
This funky hotel near Oosterpark is housed in a former orphanage dating from 1890, belying its young, fresh ambiance. Rooms are spacious, while the fixtures and fittings are simple and modern. A cafe-restaurant with a terrace overlooking the garden and a nightclub are part of the same complex. The hotel has its own private car park.

Amstel
$$$$$ 79 rooms
Prof. Tulpplein 1. 020 622 6060.
www.amstelhotel.nl.
A member of the InterContinental hotel group, this luxury hotel on the banks of the Amstel River is an Amsterdam landmark. Rooms are as sumptuous as you would expect from a hotel with the Amstel's reputation and price tag. The hotel boasts a fitness club with pool, Jacuzzi, sauna, gym and steam room. It also houses one of the Netherlands' most famous restaurants, La Rive, which specializes in French-Mediterranean cuisine. Afternoon tea from the hotel's riverside lounge is also a treat.

AMSTERDAM

INDEX

INDEX

List of Maps

Photo Credits (page Icons)

Must Know
©Blackred/iStockphoto.com *Star Attractions*: 6–11
©Luckynick/Dreamstime.com *Ideas and Tours*: 12–17
©Nigel Carse/iStockphoto.com *Calendar of Events*: 18–21
©Richard Cano/iStockphoto.com *Practical Information*: 22–23

Must Sees
©ATCB *Districts*: 38–69
©Richard Semik/age fotostock *Eternal Amsterdam*: 70–75
© Doug Olson/Fotolia.com *Cafes and Tearooms*: 76–79
©Kristen de Joseph/Michelin *All-Star Architecture*: 80–89
©Van Gogh Museum *Old Masters on View*: 90–99

©Terraxplorer/iStockphoto.com *Museums in the Mix*: 100–105
©Scott Cramer/iStockphoto.com *Parks and Gardens*: 106–109
©Sandra van der Steen/istockphoto.com *Just a Jaunt Away*: 110–115

Must Dos
©NBTC *Outdoor Activities*: 116–119
©ALEAIMAGE/iStockphoto.com *For Kids*: 120–121
©Shannon Workman/Bigstockphoto.com *Performing Arts*: 122–125
© narvikk/iStockphoto.com *Shopping*: 126–129
©Jill Chen/iStockphoto.com *Nightlife*: 130–133
©Marie-France Bélanger/iStockphoto.com *Restaurants*: 134–143
©Larry Roberg/iStockphoto.com *Hotels*: 144–153

INDEX